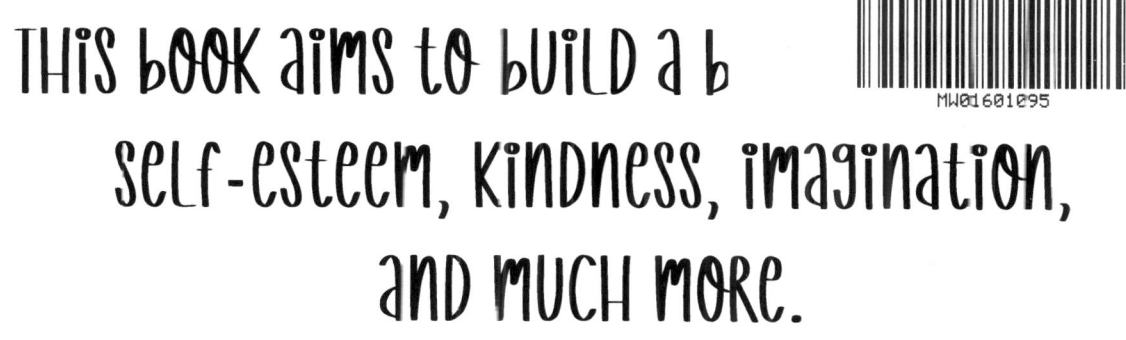

This book aims to build a b
self-esteem, kindness, imagination,
and much more.
It combines coloring with affirmation.
These coloring pages will help to build
a stronger personality and encourage
your boy to think beyond
the social conventions.

ENJOY!

Welcome

THis book belongs to:

FiRST, LeT'S geT tO KNOW YOU!

MY birthDAY is:

_____

_____

MY Biggest
secret is :

_____

_____

MY BFF is:

_____

_____

MY age is:

_____

My signature :

THIS IS A PITURE OF ME

Three things I like about myself

1.

2.

3.

FROM THIS PAGE ON, SAY ALOUD THE TEXT WRITTEN INSIDE THE BOXES. THEN COLOR THE IMAGES ON EACH PAGE.

I am Handsome

THIS PAGE IS LEFT BLANK
so you don't have to worry about the colors bleeding through
or you pressing too hard when coloring.

I am
BRAVE

I am
Bright

THIS PAGE IS LEFT BLANK
SO YOU DON'T HAVE TO WORRY ABOUT THE COLORS BLEEDING THROUGH
OR YOU PRESSING TOO HARD WHEN COLORING.

I am calm

RELAX

THIS PAGE IS LEFT BLANK
SO YOU DON'T HAVE TO WORRY ABOUT THE COLORS BLEEDING THROUGH
OR YOU PRESSING TOO HARD WHEN COLORING.

EXPLORE NEW IDEAS

I am creative

THIS PAGE IS LEFT BLANK
SO YOU DON'T HAVE TO WORRY ABOUT THE COLORS BLEEDING THROUGH
OR YOU PRESSING TOO HARD WHEN COLORING.

I am
Happy

THIS PAGE IS LEFT BLANK
SO YOU DON'T HAVE TO WORRY ABOUT THE COLORS BLEEDING THROUGH
OR YOU PRESSING TOO HARD WHEN COLORING.

I am
THOUGHTFUL

I am
strong

$5 \times 5 = \_\_$

$1 + 2 = \_$

I am smart

THIS PAGE IS LEFT BLANK
SO YOU DON'T HAVE TO WORRY ABOUT THE COLORS BLEEDING THROUGH
OR YOU PRESSING TOO HARD WHEN COLORING.

I am confident

I am
HONEST

IMAGINATION

I am
inventive

I am handsome, smart, strong, lovable, positive, confident, happy, independent, hard worker, capable, intelligent, imaginative, reliable, energetic, enough, powerful, pretty, courageous, loving, creative, clever, sweet, valuable, vibrant, amazing, optimistic, fabulous, kind, thankful, honest, organized, patient, friendly, peaceful, humble.

THIS PAGE IS LEFT BLANK
SO YOU DON'T HAVE TO WORRY ABOUT THE COLORS BLEEDING THROUGH
OR YOU PRESSING TOO HARD WHEN COLORING.

I am all of this and so much more

THIS PAGE IS LEFT BLANK
so you don't have to worry about the colors bleeding through
or you pressing too hard when coloring.

I want to be a

....

WHEN I GROW UP.

NOW I CAN COLOUR THE FOLLOWING
DRAWINGS AND CUT THEM OUT
TO KEEP THEM WITH ME
FOR A LONG TIME. . .

DOCTOR

THIS PAGE IS LEFT BLANK
so you don't have to worry about the colors bleeding through
or you pressing too hard when coloring.

Astronaut

THIS PAGE IS LEFT BLANK
SO YOU DON'T HAVE TO WORRY ABOUT THE COLORS BLEEDING THROUGH
OR YOU PRESSING TOO HARD WHEN COLORING.

ARTIST

COWBOY

Sportsman

scientist

singer

THIS PAGE IS LEFT BLANK
SO YOU DON'T HAVE TO WORRY ABOUT THE COLORS BLEEDING THROUGH
OR YOU PRESSING TOO HARD WHEN COLORING.

BUILDER

THIS PAGE IS LEFT BLANK
so you don't have to worry about the colors bleeding through
or you pressing too hard when coloring.

Thank you

We hope you liked this coloring book.

We would love to hear your feedback and suggestions
for future revisions. Contact us on the web at:

www.mytprint.com.au

Post photos of your completed pages online with hash tag #mytprint
or email us at: contest@mytprint.com.au
We would love to feature your work and you could win our monthly drawing!

While you are there,
join our mailing list for FREE downloadable samples
and checkout our new releases and monthly promotions.
(PS: We don't share or spam your email. Promise!)

And please consider leaving a review, there is no obligation
but it would be appreciated and will also help us grow.

MYTPrint

Macramé

Transform Your Home & Garden with This Complete Step By Step Macramé Book for Beginners and Creative Challenges for Experts, 70 Stunning, Easy and Modern Illustrated Patterns and Projects

by

Gretchen Crafts

Macramè

TABLE OF CONTENTS

Macramè

Introduction

Macramé is the way of making textiles that use knots instead of techniques of knitting or weaving. Macramé has also been used by boaters to decorate objects on their boats and is often used to make shoes, containers, blankets, hangers for plants, and hangings for walls. Usually, suede and leather are utilized to make friendship bracelets, and macramé also used to build the macramé belts created by many people.

There is a huge variety of variations of knots or knots methods used for macramé along with the half knot, square knot, half hitch, the head knot of the larks, and the coil knot. Many different patterns may be made, based on the usage of knots and how they're used individually or in conjunction with others.

Cords are basically available in different thicknesses ranging from .5 to 8 mm. The larger the number, the thicker the cord, so 8 mm is the thickest. We can often use rings and beads crafted from silicone. A project is most easily worked on a flat macramé board. The project is carried out using t-pins, which aid in arranging the patterns of knots.

There is a large range of colors, fabrics, and cord forms suitable for use in macramé, some synthetic and some natural. Indeed, almost everything where you could tie knots might be appropriate, and elements can be available in various places like hardware, craft, bricolage, sewing stores, and needlework. In some instances, the material chosen may be determined by what is going to be produced while, in some, it will be important to play with your decisions because while there are cords widely utilized with some tasks, that does not mean that some others do not perform quite as well.

Some examples of cords which can be used in macramé consist of:

- Nylon
- Rayon
- Waxed cotton
- Silk
- Hemp
- Rattail
- Polypropylene
- Leather
- Wool
- Crochet thread
- Suede
- Stick thread

While deciding a material to have for a task, it is necessary to think about finished pieces, and how these should be used, as few might be more functional or practical. Stiff, dense cords are always not the right option for jewelry design, but they may be suitable for a grocery bag that wants to bear any mass and not quickly tear or wear. If several cord forms are ideal for a task, they may end up in very different finished products. A jewelry style crafted from the delicate cotton cord, for example, would be lighter, smoother, and more secure than the same item made from a hard/thick leather cord. One thing to remember about the length of the strings is how simple it is to use them. Thicker cords may be simpler because when they're tight, certain styles are hard to hold the knots to their place. Light cords can work fiddly and painfully, but the final product can be fantastic and quite accurate.

Chapter 1: A Fascinating Macramé History and Tradition

When many people think about macramé, they imagine the results of the upsurge in the popularity of the textile technique during the 1970s — contraptions for hanging glass and plant tabletops, multi-tiered lampshades, and belts, pockets, and other Bohemian-favored accessories. Although macramé blends in with many developments from the period — the perfect way to put a piping hot fondue pot on top of a macramé doily, obvs — the roots reach back thousands of years across oceans.

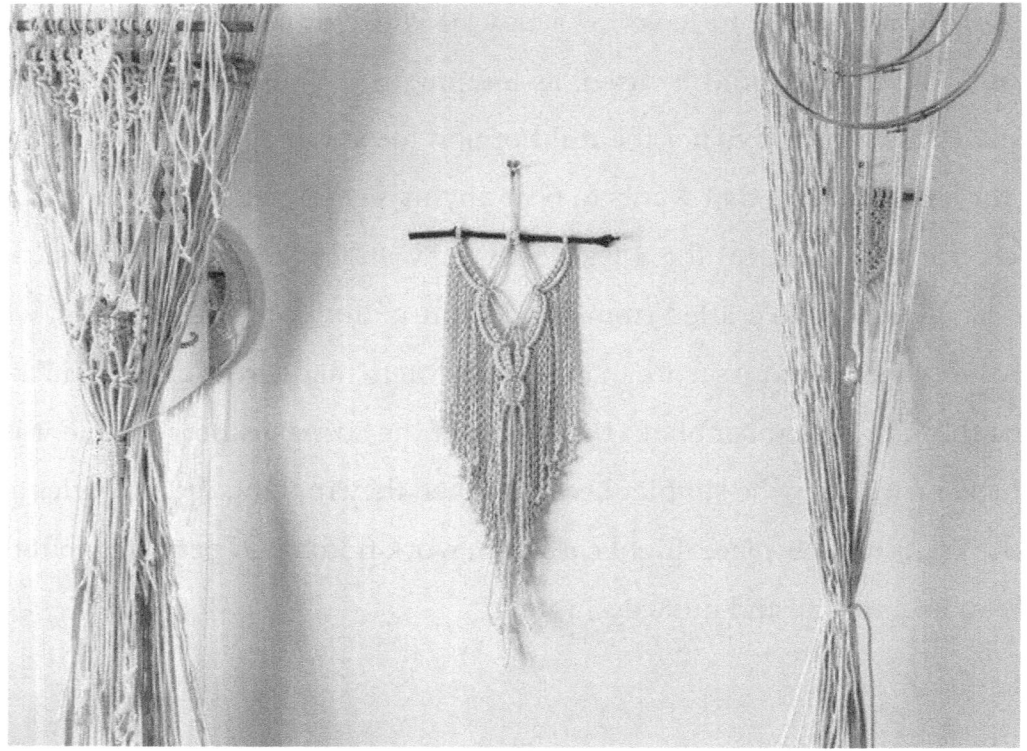

Many claims that the name "macramé" derives from the Arabic word migramah or "fringe." A first recorded "macraméers," were Arabic weavers from the 13th century, who started to attach decorative knots to protect the loose ends of woven textiles, such as towels and shawls. (Others believe that the phrase comes from the Turkish word makrama, relating to napkins and towels that used the knotting method in a similar fashion.) Irrespective of where and when macramé received its name, the technique is just as old as its simple structure: a knot that has an almost endless number of variants, innumerable functional applications and produced an unknown number of headaches.

Macramé, like other fiber crafts, is mostly favored by women these days, however, to be more precise, some of the most prominent and successful macraméers were people — sailors. Knowing the versatility of the simple reef knot (or square knot) and the power of various hook knots to tie sails and fill cargo with ropes, the early maritime explorers learned that knot-tying could also relieve their boredom. These sailors also started binding for months on end at sea, incorporating more intricate knots into elegant designs for occasional functional applications, such as bell pulls and rope ladders. As the ships docked at different locations, often the sailors would sell or barter their jobs, and the macramé art — and the popularization of nautical products such as rope and twine — began to expand to many nations, including China, in what was then known as "the New World."

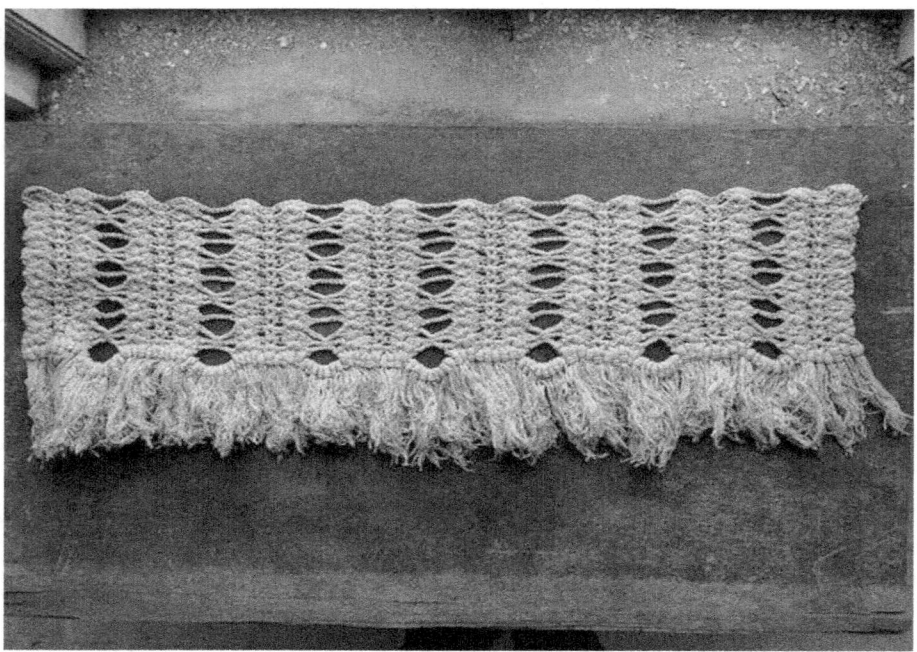

Sailors were not the only evangelists with a macramé. The Moors contributed Spain to the Arab knot-tying method, which they used until the fifteenth century, and it gradually found its way to France and Italy. Queen Mary II of England taught her ladies-in-waiting how to macramé in the 17th century; almost 200 years later, during Queen Victoria's reign and the subsequently called Victorian Period, the art form became all the rage. Macramé information adorned anything from floral centerpieces to curtains and bedspreads, which was a common activity for females of the period.

The popularity of Macramé faded in the early 1900s, and although it did not completely disappear, for over half a century, the craft became far more obscure both in commodities and in practice. Later, in the 1970s, people started unexpectedly going crazy again for knots.

Macramé's return at the height of the feminist revolution represented a wider societal dichotomy — on the one side, many of these people buckled conventional social norms, such as marriage and motherhood, in search of independent equality and their financial and sexual freedoms; on the other, in their spare time, they resurrected an art that achieved peak success in an epoch renowned for its Only they had a wild, over-the-top, uninhibited and grandiose approach to the craft. In the 1970s, it was crafted from macramé and could be just about all you might picture.

The era's biggest macramé phenomenon has been, yeah, a true hoot. The macramé owl's past, one of the most omnipresent and absurd images of the art, is a little enigmatic. Owls were a common subject in home decor in the 1970s, and the pattern could be linked to the United States. In 1971, the announcement by the Forest Service to appoint Woodsy Owl as their logo. The character wore a red-feathered Robin Hood-esque green cap and urged people to "give a hoot, don't pollute!" Owls are often deemed magical beings in many societies, symbolizing knowledge and bringing good luck; they are among the most important animals in Feng Shui, the ancient Chinese tradition that seeks to use energy powers to establish peace between humans and their climate. Following President Richard Nixon's iconic trip to China in 1972, Feng Shui was extremely marketable in the U.S., and it was prime material for the increasing New Age movement.

In 1977, the former Home magazine of the Los Angeles Times not only ventured out the macramé owl as THE must-have home decor piece but also marketed a $7.95 DIY package. Thousands of once-treasured macramé owls were discarded as macramé went out of favor again in the early 80s. The survivors are still to be found in thrift shops and on Etsy, looking just as dumb as the day they were born.

Macramé all but vanished during the 1980s, 1990s, and '00s as a home decor phenomenon, but the art has made a gradual return in the last five years. Modern bohemianism includes not just fashion and home design, but a whole lifestyle centered on personal growth, spiritual advancement, and the value of "self-care" practice, particularly for women. Hobbies with a feminine heritage, including fiber arts such as macramé, have sparked interest; thanks to Instagram, Etsy, Pinterest, and other social and e-commerce platforms, modern macramé has sparked interest;

1.1 What macramé actually is?

Macramé might be the moment's millennial DIY but it goes back decades!

Macramé is all over the place! At a yoga center, you don't have to go far away for the workshop to teach a person about how to sew a knotty hanging board, a simple key chain, or a drapey plant hanger together. Minimalist and Boho combinations make for a hot but amazing look. If you've recently embellished your house with it, either it's a project of DIY, or choose an already produced piece from the even TJ Maxx, or flea market, your parents, might be amazed on their visit to your house. How did the 21st century discover fresh life in this often-maligned product of the '70s? They asked, and we replied.

There, the thing with something that comes back from the furniture of the '70s is that architecture wasn't an especially prosperous moment. Whole rooms were devoted to green avocado, from the furniture to the curtains to the walls, rounding it out with the impact of the gold crop. Yuck! And though certain colors are growing stay throughout the 1970s, macramé is back, offering white walls with soothing texture, and floating throughout comparison to green plants.

Defined Macramé

It is the style of textile produced using techniques of knotting, as opposed to kneading or weaving. The macramé knots are double half-hitch and full-hitch, square, and shape. The art only needed inexpensive and affordable materials such as hemp, cotton twine, leather, or wool, with specific beads utilized to improve the item.

Macramé's first accounts are attributed to Arab Weavers of the 13th century; they used extra threads to make knotted beautifully decorated threads patterns on handmade cloth. China of the third century is also attributed gratitude to the pan shift knot — a set of loops that converge into patterns of infinity to signify immortality. Sailors were also a major supportive character of the craft's origins in the amazing Era of Sail, in the 1700s until around 1830, Knots were used by them to blast their blades, cans, and ship pieces, whilst their understanding of different forms of knots was utilized to barter wisdom!

Macramé became the common textile that developed into placemats, tassels, picture frames, plant slings in the corner, wall hangings, hammocks, and even bikinis; the '70s took on the ornate rope work trend.

Though enthusiasm languishes after the 1970s, a revived interest in DIY tutorials on personal pages for bloggers and YouTube has recently sparked off. We're just on the train for crafternoons, right?

Apartment tenants consider macramé especially appealing because of its potential to convert the most of the house hanging plants in their room as a solution to the need of a yard or garden, and a way of getting the world in with more no of buildings rising up and chopping down trees (you can also check out this indoor hanging herb garden). So, you can acknowledge the history of past centuries for motivating yourself for craft attack the next time your mother and father wonder why you've gone macramé crazy.

1.2 Modern macramé

Knot, braid, tie: the modern way to unwind: Macramé has been out for a long time ago, now it is celebrating a fantastic bounce back as an indoor trend. It develops from Germany via New York and London to Tokyo, and it can be found once again in the unique concept stores and in famous restaurants. Macramé tsunami has swamped the beauty forums completely with directions for knotting. Therefore, DIY-lovers with smart fingers tie a knot above knot in living rooms around the world and turn every space into a glamorous gallery with its macramé tapestries and plant hangers.

Old design formulas also have a way to unwind.

So, why do we like macramé? This, traditional textile manufacturing, hand-knotted type? The internet age has transformed our daily lives dramatically and led to, among other factors, a profound shift in customer behavior. There are indicators of a shift at a distance of the digital environment to physical objects, which could be seen in both architecture, construction, interiors and lifestyle, food, and fashion. And many people are already waiting to do it again. A new wave of « Do it on your own » was formed through the trend of « Do it on your own,» powered by the thousands, also called the

Y generation. We want natural products and special objects. One consequence in the world of interiors is the famous bounce back of macramé, the craft of knotting from hand textiles. The beauty is that macramé takes a lot of energy, quiet, and implementation, and it has something contemplative that generation Y is sorely missing.

A group that embraces inner peace

Group Y takes its own special direction in the finding for harmony and inner peace. Like a counter-direction against immediacy, the motto is unwinding. The fundamental prerequisite is that of a balance of work-life. The big return of this macramé is not even so shocking from this viewpoint. Among others at the forefront of this trend is the Sally England, an American artist for textile who since 2010 has focused completely on this old practice and rediscovered the elegance of knotting. With her macramé pieces of art in a large format with an extremely modern look, she has catapulted the conventional handicrafts into the here and now. Her works represent the need for individuality, natural resources, and unwindingness of our culture. She blends all great technological know-how with Generation Y's fun spontaneity. This fresh, Bohemian chic hippy trend is spreading like a plague across the globe. Many other macramé skilled artists like Lise Silva with macramé necklaces made by her or maybe the German visionary Dörte Bundt having her workshops are training our vision for a different kind of biodiversity and patrimony.

The macramé founder-Sally England

Sally, England is simply heading the latest « Hippy age 2.0 mark » with the macramé wave. She was born in Ann Arbor in 1979 and lived her youth surrounded by magical streams, woods, and plains. In this, she found a profound connection with nature.

Maturing in a 2nd-generation artist household, at a young age, her tactile passion for textiles and natural fabrics was already awoken. She read as a teenager, a novel on macramé, which was her mother's. She finished her bachelor's degree in « Arts Communication » first, then started researching old macramé published books as a side hand, driven by her respect for traditional handicraft processes, and in doing so, she carried out great research into the old knotting technique. Sally England moved to her homeland of Michigan after this and opened a workshop in the ancient Victorian flat. Far from a big city's quick tempo, she has chosen this her platform to pay attention to the macramé's meditative, time-intensive work processes. Unique tools for her are her hands. She does ordinary works from dense ropes on the one hand, and also room dividers and large-scale sculptural tapestries on the other. This led to modern representations with remarkable tactility, including abstract patterns, linear circles, and intricate structures. In her series called « Black Gold,» she mixed items such as loam, gold, and leather into and about the raw cotton cord. Meanwhile, her macramé creations have gained global prominence and can be seen in numerous galleries like New York's « R20th Century Architecture Gallery ». Magazines like « The Chicago Tribune » and « The Wall Journal » have positively written on her job, and her clientele includes prominent names such as Tommy Hilfiger, Ralph Lauren, Luxury Hotel ACE in London, or the Nike. It is because they are both influenced by the latest generation of macramé.

The knotting art

The past of macramé began in the 13th century at the time when intricate, hand-knotted decoration heads were made by Arab weavers to shield their horses from flying objects and decorate their homes. The trade may, however, often be traced back to the Freemasons and Crusaders. The macramé painting traveled from Spain and Italy all over the globe on 15th-century sailing ships. During the long voyages at sea, sailors knotted nets, hanging mats, and gifts for their beloved ones in the place of the different port where they land. Nevertheless, during the era of Victorians, macramé was undergoing its golden age. In the 1960s, as hippies adorned their skirts, plant hangers, and waistcoats with fringes, this ancient practice underwent a second revival, railing opposite to the way the environment was changing and through knotting for harmony. Throughout the chic, innovative 1980s, marked by the Cold War, T-shirts made of knots and vibrant friendship bracelets sparked a fleeting return of conventional knotting techniques.

Now macramé's making a critical comeback! And it honors the elegance of wasting time knotting, with its latest style of interior accessories. This breathed fresh vitality and attention into the old culture. Via macramé, we again reflect on making enough time for necessary stuff in life. This offers us a chance in a fast-digital age to think calmly about everything.

Chapter 2: Getting started in macramé

Macramé is the technique of ancient Arab weaver used to design decorative fringes on things such as veils, shawls, and towels for baths. Today, this knotting method is used to create ties, wall hangers, plant hangers, and jewelry. Intricate, one-of-a-kind designs may be realized with preparation. To get going, Macramé needs a few inexpensive devices.

2.1 Tools required for macramé

Macramé Project Board

A project mounting board is a principal device required for macramé. The board is the working area where it secures the work. At art shops, you can find boards with grid inch markings and fitting directions written on the fronts. A project board may, therefore, be rendered by gluing together or using cork foam sheets. The board may be suitable for a macramé project so long as it is thick enough to prevent the nails from sticking out the back.

T-Nails

T-Nails are used to secure onto the mounting board the macramé yarn or rope. T-nails come out in various sizes. Smaller nails are ideal for smaller, more delicate designs. Nails appear to break following prolonged use. Those built of steel are more durable and can maintain for longer use.

Pattern

Many things can be created with macramé — from purses to infant mobiles. A handy-tool is a macramé template. Macramé patterns provide step-by-step guidance on the knots to be used, directions for calculating, and guidelines for final assembly. Buy patterns, or you will search them online.

Scissors

A decent pair of sharp scissors could be used to cut threads correctly on a macramé layout. There are different sizes and comfort grips. Consider purchasing the sort to cover the blades with a sheath protector.

Tweezers

Another device used for the decoration function is tweezers. You can use a pair of tweezers to help good knot threads between the bead-work.

Needles

In fact, needles are used for macramé. Needles are used for the alignment of the completed product and for perforation. Depending on the inclination are used blunt-end or tapestry needles and Chenille or pointed needles. Specific measurements are used to fit yarn styles like silk or nylon, and for different formed beads.

2.2 Tips for beginners

It's such an amazing feeling to discover macramé and get inspired to learn, but it can also be daunting when you sit down and trying to figure out how to start.

Begin with Simple Knots

There are too many different knots to know if you're new to the game, which can seem overwhelming. To get the methodology down, we recommend you begin with a few simple patterns and knots. A decent first to know knot is a basic knot in a rectangle. These days, this knot is the very foundation of much of the macramé out there, and a surprisingly simple knot for beginners to try. This knot is the one all learn in our workshops!

Attend A Workshop

Educating yourself is enjoyable, but I recommend you attend a workshop if you have any in your city. You get to interact with too many like-minded individuals and also depart not just with your own finished artwork but even with new mates.

Save Your Left-Over Chord

As you're practicing, there might be a handful of attempts you're going to fight back. And getting the right JUST rope length can be your biggest barrier. You never want to have little rope because attaching extra to your piece can be complicated. We also recommend that you make at least 10 percent more errors than you think you should, just to be healthy.

We have a comprehensive step-by-step calculation in the latest Modern Macramé book on how to decide how much rope you need for your macramé!

This is in mind; at the end of your project, maybe you wind up with extra rope! But don't think! We suggest that you save every rope leftover. You should recycle the recycled rope into potential designs.

Study Online

If you can't see us at a laboratory in person, viewing videos online is the second-best thing. Often, it's easier to follow someone who shows you the ropes, rather than reading instructions on a page. There are many tutorials on YouTube.

Have Fun

One of the best aspects of the trip is sharing your imagination through Macramé! Don't be too hard on yourself. T Let your imagination take the lead, and you'll end up with a beautiful product.

Further tips will explain it better:

1. Study the simple hemp rope knots, because it's quick to deal with and easy to remove knots.
2. Using nylon ropeing for your initial jewelry designs, rather than silk, until you have the simple macramé knots down. The removal of knotting errors is even simpler.
3. Singing the ends just fits for roping in nylon.
4. Create a basic project board that can be used as your workspace. Made it simple, and can go everywhere, makes your project really portable. A sealed envelope, corkboard, or just a sheet of polyurethane foam will be dense so that nails won't fall through.
5. Double test also that the rope you want to use suits through the bead holes (before starting!)
6. Only attach a knot at the end of the rope to prevent the ends from fraying.

7. Clear nail polish on the ends of the ropes can also be used to keep them from fraying, and this also stiffens the ends, allowing to string those tiny seed beads. A "no-fray" liquid found in fabric stores can also be used to do the same job.

8. Save left roping pieces to learn new ties on.

9. For your piece, the secret to a finished look is standardized knotting. Practice makes things perfect!

10. If not nails are on deck, using the corsage nails to protect your job. Create an x with two nails to lock the rope in position so as not to puncture the thread by utilizing leather roping. Place the nails diagonally on each side of the cable, like an X to keep the cable in place.

2.3 Macramé supplies

To build the craft projects, Macramé supplies and crafts equipment is required. There is a list of the specific things that you need below before beginning any project.
Many markets and hardware stores hold stocks of art if you don't have such things at home already.

You'll need a table or some other surface to function.
Working away from home on your idea, a clipboard not only keeps the ropes but also offers you a solid surface to operate on.
Safety Tip: Make sure you have a clean and uncluttered work surface. Keep ropes away from food, drinks, and cigarettes.
The ropes used during Macramé are often very long, so when they become caught in them, they can hurt pets so small children.
Seek to bring all your resources into some sort of quick to transport organizer.

To keep the nails or tape you would require a Project Panel.

Cardboard, clipboards, Styrofoam and poster boards can be included.

Furthermore, ceiling tiles and foam parts work, as do strong pillows.

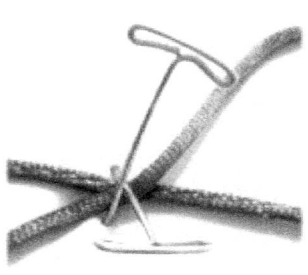

To attach the ties to the project frame, t-nails or strong sewing nails are required, so ensure you have enough.

The cross-nail method seen here is a perfect way to use nails to lock fragile ropes without reaching around the ropes.

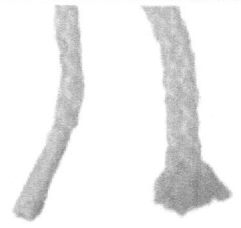

Cellophane rolls and masking tape are useful, and can be preserved alongside the other Macramé materials.

As seen below, you should put tape on the tips of ropes to keep them from unraveling.

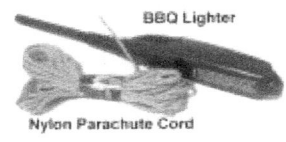

Do you use synthetic materials, like nylon rope Parachute?

If you intend to fire up the ropes you may require a BBQ Lighter.

For specifics see Rope Preparedness.

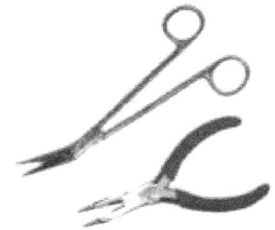

A pair of small, sharp scissors will be required.

Fine tip pliers, tweezers (or surgical clamps), particularly if you're using beads or fine ropes, are suggested too.

For several Macramé projects, a flexible measurement tape is required.

It is easy to use fabric and/or household glue both for painting and planning, so make sure to have some handy.

See to it that the adhesive dries transparent (not white).

 Natural materials may require a beeswax coating, which maintains and softens the fibers.

 For jewelry, you would require 1 mm-2 mm string products.

 Beads, pendants, and clasps Micro-Macramé can also be required.

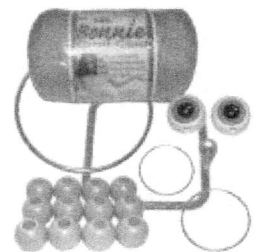 Macramé suppliers need 3 mm-6 mm rope material for regular sized ventures.

Can often include macramé beads, circles, animal eyes, and other objects.

2.4 Selecting a macramé chord

If you are new to macramé, as I was once, you can always find yourself doing a lot of work on the topic of macramé ronailg. I find discriminating between all the various forms of macramé rope out there and which one I would use may be frustrating.

In this article, we're going to go into great depth on the topic of macramé rope, and by the end of the section, you should have a good idea of the various forms of macramé rope, and it's the intent. Let's start by describing what rope is macramé.

Macramé rope is a group of twisted or braided fibers/strands which are then used to bind or knot together to form a textile art known as macramé.

Many of you who are just starting will also read or hear the macramé rope is often referred to as macramé thread, wire, or lines. Of these synonyms,' macramé rope is sometimes used interchangeably.

New beginners can find it challenging to learn what each term implies, so let's take a deeper dive into the macramé rope and the various types of ropes you should care about. Thus, you can choose the right rope for your future macramé projects.

When I first began macramé, I had no idea that various rope styles existed. I thought the macramé string was just plain-Jane rope, and that was what macramé really requiring. I didn't know that there were all kinds of fibers that can be used in your projects. At the time, I knew very little, not all macramé ropes are made equal.

Let's take them down. Macramé's three main rope styles are:

- Braided
- 3-ply/3 Strand
- Single Strand

Most of the macramé designs you find online may always fall into either of these types.

Macramé Braided Rope

Braided string or even named Macramé rope is the standard macramé string you'll find in the big box department shops, Hobby Lobby, Michaels, and also Wal-Mart.

Most macramé beginners should start by buying braided rope because it's the simplest and most inexpensive way to start macramé. It is typically available in most specialty shops and broad box retailers as braided thread. Most citizens rush to their nearest store to buy any chord they may locate because they want to get going immediately. After finishing a few macramé tasks, they can discover easily that braided rope is not the most appropriate form of rope for macramé creation. This is because the braided rope is essentially individually made up of rope, or a combination of cotton, nylon, polyester, polypropylene, or other strong fibers. Tying stuff together and having it a firm grip is fine, but it's hard to un-knot and fringe with.

With that being said, it's no poor way to continue using a braided rope. It gets the job finished, and you will wind up with a product that has been decently completed. More frequently than not, you're likely to find yourself switching to either a 3-ply or the more widely used macramé string-a single line.

Usage of macramé rope and string can also be seen. They are usually asking about something specific. How I discern between the two is that rope is usually braided, or 3-ply rope and rope is an all-encompassing concept for fibers, ropes, and rope.

Macramé 3-Ply / 3-Stands Rope

The 3-ply rope is also regarded as the 3-stand cable. It consists of three smaller threads to create a wide twisted rope. You will also hear macramé artists speaking of utilizing 3-ply or 4-ply macramé rope, indicating the number of twisted threads connected to create a single strand of string. Below you can see the gap between the 3-Ply and 4-Ply visually.

When you venture into macramé ropes, which are more than three fibers, that's what's called multi-ply, where you may get 4, 5, or 6-strands twisted all together to shape one string. As you can see from the first picture above, four strands are twisted together in order to shape a single strand of rope.

Macramé Single Strand Rope

Single strand cotton string is by far the best form of macramé rope to pick from as a daily hobby or full-time job. Single strand rope is usually more costly, and even if you don't want to splurge on a pricey rope right now, find some inexpensive cotton rope on amazon and start with those. As long as it's easy on the hands, learning from it would be fine. It would make cutting rope, joining ties, unraveling ties, and fringing the string a lot simpler.

Now that you have an idea of the three different forms of macramé rope, let's speak about four main points on what you can check for while selecting which macramé rope to use for your macramé ventures.

Macramé Rope Composition

Natural or Synthetic Fiber

Macramé rope make-up breaks into two sections, natural or synthetic fibers.

Animal fibers are also naturally generated fibers. They are created by growing plants, livestock, or geology. Examples of natural fibers include cotton, linen, jute, hemp, and wool.

All such fibers can be broken down and recycled naturally.

The other option is one of the synthetic fibers. The synthetic fibers are constructed from tiny molecular synthesized polymers. The substances used to produce such fabrics come from raw materials like chemicals dependent on petroleum, called petrochemicals. Nylon, polyester, and spandex are representatives of the synthetic fibers.

Macramé Rope Texture

Macramé feel, touch, appearance, finish, and texture

When you've seen a range of macramé ropes, you'll find that each spool of rope has a particular look, finish, and texture. Having a grasp of the various rope texture styles is a vital aspect of having to learn the macramé ropes.

For all of your macramé designs, the more macramé parts you create, the faster you can find texture plays a huge role.

If you are going to make a purchase online on macramé rope, seek various suppliers of products to see which quality suits you. You can note that not all cotton ropes made of macramé are made equal. The texture and sound of the ropes will differ from supplier to supplier.

Macramé Rope Size

Length and diameter

It's also really necessary to know the chord size while making your ideal macramé project. Rope scale plays a crucial function in the artistic presentation of macramé designs.

On the sizes of macramé ropes, we should not go into great depth. If you are curious, we have another article going into the different sizes of macramé rope. I use what Type of Macramé rope for my designs.

For convenience, rope macramé can be broken down into groups of 3 sizes – thin, medium, and huge.

1. Small Macramé Rope- The chord is usually 1-2 mm in diameter. These strings are also used to create jewelry thread by beads and buttons and in small-detailed art projects.

2. Medium Macramé Rope-is where most of the macramé ventures are produced. Usually, that ranges from 3mm-5 mm. You'll often go for 3 mm or 4 mm, more commonly. Such measurements are also used for hangers to trees, hangings to doors, lanterns, curtains, rugs, etc.

3. Large Macramé Rope-This will be your bits of BIG macramé. This will be in the 6 mm and above the class of something. These large sizes are normally used to cover large areas of space. You may note that the ties appear to be less but much wider.

What Macramé Rope Do You Use?

The easiest explanation is: This depends.

For me personally, I would suggest using Single Strand Cotton Rope 3mm-4 mm. If you've done a lot of projects utilizing a cheaper rope and now, you're confident spending in some nicer rope for higher quality projects, then a single strand rope could be right for you. If you're a brand-new novice and want to continue using the perfect rope right now, you can do it, too, by all chance.

The purpose I'd consider using a single strand rope is that it will boost your experience with macramé. It will be less of a struggle to tie knots and unravel them. Cutting ropes and fringing won't seem like hard-working, and most notably, the macramé creations would be aesthetically appealing to come out.

Macramé Beginners / Occasional Knotters

I realize not everybody on their macramé path is at the same point, and my advice does not extend to everybody. If you're new to this profession, I'd suggest to practice using some rope that you've laid around. If not, grab a cheap rope from the nearest design shop if you want to get going instantly or get some from amazon. This Amazon cable is greater than the rope you'll find at your nearest design shop. Using this rope to learn the curls, designs, and sequences of macramé binding. To get you going, this is the most cost-effective macramé chain. Start by creating smaller macramé tasks such as key chains or feather patterns using macramé to get a feel for creating the knots.

Macramé Lovers & Enthusiasts

I will suggest high quality 3mm-4 mm single strand cotton rope for those of you looking to create your macramé knotting techniques and to highlight your designs.

Alongside the effortless fringing, the smooth feel and simplicity of knotting allow the use of the best form of macramé rope. I use it for 99 percent of my designs for macramé. Bochiknot Macramé online sells the best grade cotton string macramé. If you're keen to get started on macramé designs, there'll be plenty of rope to get you moving with one spool of 3 mm single strand yarn.

One spool of macramé rope might be able to get you 2 to 3 projects of medium size macramé. If you are looking for just a little more, so you don't run out of macramé rope, two spools would be more than sufficient to cover current and future macramé projects.

Things to consider while selecting a rope

1. Composition-very important is the material from which the macramé rope was made. Fibers like hemp and jute were once quite popular with macramé artists.

However, their industry development motivated the increase in popularity of nylon and satin ray-made macramé strings, which are man-made fibers. I recommend you use nylon as a novice since it's simple to undo in case you create a knotting mistake.

2. Power-A macramé rope's power primarily depends on its structure. A rope made of jute, cotton, rope, and nylon is sturdy enough.

3. Twist – The strength of the rope is calculated by the twisting or braiding of the individual strands of the thread during the production phase. A braided macramé rope is less simple to undo than a twisted string.

Often handle the ends of a chord before beginning a macramé project so as to avoid the stands from splitting. The ends may be coated in molten translucent wax.

If you want to build a fringe, guarantee that the threads do not break past the duration of the fringe by knotting the top of the fringe.

4. Stiffness-A rope should be versatile enough to curl and stretch acropeing to the specifications of the design. When you are creating a bracelet or necklace, it is preferred to use a thinner macramé chain. An embroidery rope made from cotton, for example,

is smooth and very durable. You may also use cloth; just make sure that the width is less than 2 mm.

5. Texture – There are macramé ropes that feel rough and which may irritate the skin. Necklaces and bracelets are not recommended for making hemp and metal ropes. Suggested materials were nylon, silk, satin rayon, and cotton. You can also use leather because after a period of use it softens.

6. The diameter or width-The macramé rope thickness is usually indicated in millimeters (mm). Bear in mind when buying a rope, whether they can be inserted into beads, buttons, or other decorations.

Ropes with diameters of more than 4.0 mm may require larger decorations. A good-sized rope should have a diameter of less than 2.0 mm for making micro-macramé projects, such as bracelets and necklaces.

7. Quantity or amount – The amount of the rope is the length of the rope required for the whole project. Many cables come in big rolls, and others come in shorter lengths. Many people use ropes of nylon and cloth as they search for most of the finest macramé artists' values. Personally, I prefer these two rope types, because they are also available on the market.

Linhasitha rope- pros and cons

This string is probably from Peru. Linhasita was the second rope I had used for my projects with macramé. It is a very flexible and robust rope that lies between C-Lon rope and Thai wax rope in terms of user-friendliness and appearance. It doesn't have the glamorous shine that C-Lon rope offers, but it definitely creates some good-looking bits because the ties are quite straight when bound with this rope. Because of its wax content, the rope itself feels a little stiff but is still workable. It is ideal for every project involving macramé. It's not as readily accessible as C-Lon rope or Chinese wax rope, but there are few reputable outlets that can bring this rope to you. Its thickness of 1 mm ensures no seed beads smaller than 8/0 (3 mm) are threadable. All and all, for beginners and experienced macramé artists alike, this is a perfect rope, and I will suggest this cable.

Pros:

• Linhasita designs are very robust, and can even get damp without losing form or light.

• The string is produced in a rather straightforward way, delivering outstanding outcomes.

• Linhasita strings come in different colors. A strong collection is available that will allow a great range of colors in your projects.

• Spools spanning 180m/195 yards give reasonable value for energy.

• It is UV and mildew resistant

• Due to the wax quality of the ropes, no adhesives are needed to finish the projects

Cons:

• While I like Linhasita's look, it doesn't deliver the sleek and even looks of unbraided wax ropes.

• It's a little sticky and makes undoing poor ties a little harder. Kumihimo designs often operate with this rope, but as longer ropes tangle, it may get a little difficult.

• If caution is not taken to hold the ends away from the floor or dirty surfaces when knotting, the soil can easily bind to this rope.

2.5 Difference between a string, rope, and rope

Macramé String is the smooth, single twist string that Niroma Studio always began as you know it today. It's the product I made for my own use to create my own macramé wall hangings because at the time I couldn't find it anywhere in the U.S. And because of its softness and the beautiful fringe it makes, it is what I believe so many people have evolved to love for.

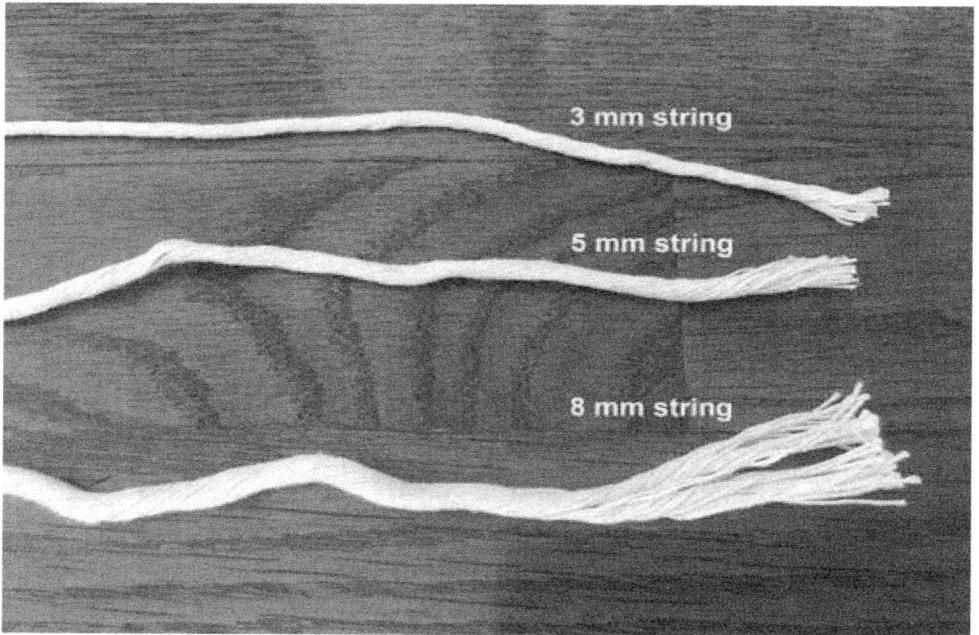

I sell it in natural cotton of 3 mm, 5 mm, and 7 mm, and my Super soft line is a single twist row too.

* * A short sizing note * * * The dimensions I send was after the string was cut and had the opportunity to stretch. String stretches faster than string or thread because it unwinds quickly such that the total width will range from 1 to 1.5 mm from when firmly wounded along the conduit to when splitting and breathable. Other retailers can mark something special, so keep that in mind.

"What's the right macramé string for beginners?" I always get questioned, and I always choose the 5 mm natural cotton string. It is the right size to hang a nice medium-sized wall, and it fits better than the 3 mm, plus it has a very compact medium twist on it, and it can be gently unknotted and reknotted a couple of times before losing its credibility as long as you are conscious. And being gentle on the hands of course always tends to keep you moving!

Macramé Rope is typically a 3-strand rope where the fibers are wrapped around each other (sometimes called a 3-ply). I saw it in four strands, but traditional rope appears to be three strands. Macramé rope is usually stronger than macramé string, and it gives you the nice, wavy fringe when you untwist it, so it's perfect for adding dimension to your job.

Since it is heavier, I like to use it for parts of items that would have to carry considerable weight. Macramé rope often stretches when it has been cut, so depending on where you stay, how much humidity you have, etc... it will also stretch up to 1 cm. Macramé Rope is typically a 6-strand (or more) braided thread, or what I believe was more widely used for macramé in the 1970s so early 1980s when the cotton string wasn't exactly 'the thing' to use. The really, really tightly woven cotton macramé rope is sometimes called "sash rope." Sash rope is a little rigid to use and quite hard to remove, yet it's incredibly solid, so it's perfect for weight-bearing parts and if you're trying to add plenty of strength to your job. In my experience, Macramé rope is the worst on hands, but when you want a certain look or versatility, there's no discomfort, no cost!

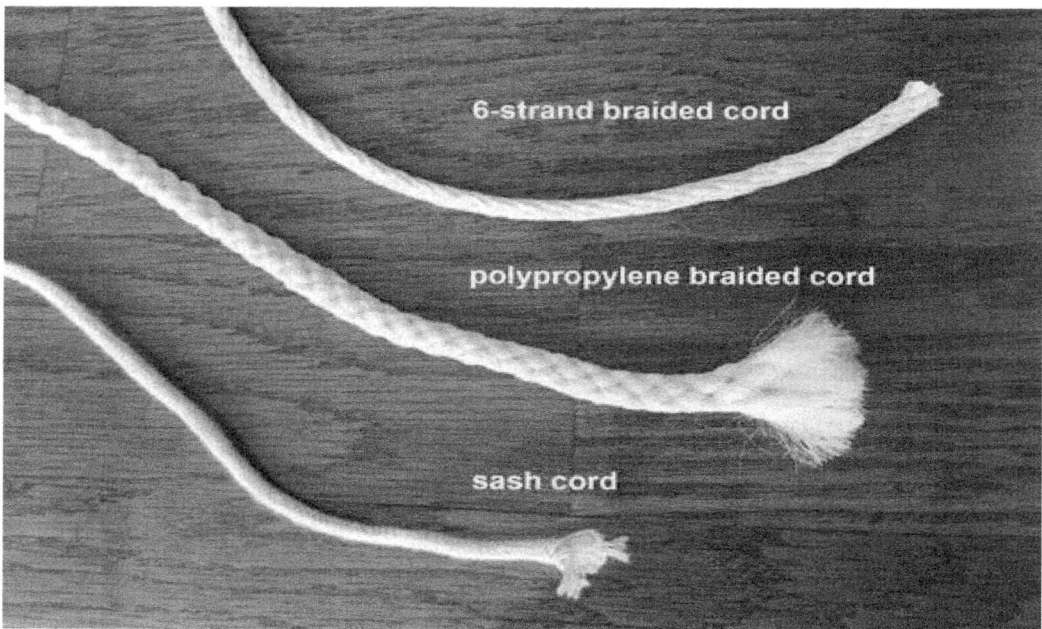

Then there is polypropylene (or polyolefin) macramé rope, some of you may recognize one labeled variant as Bonnie Design String, which is perfect for outdoor usage because it does not shape because easily as cotton. The edge can be "frizzy," and that's only something to hold in mind.

2.6 How to start a macramé project?

It's the craft/art of binding ropes into knots in a way as they create a decorative or useful shape. Selecting the best fabrics and double-check you have a decent workroom can help you off the project correctly. Next, master the simple macramé knots. The reverse lark's knot (head) is wherewith you'll launch most designs. Square and Half knots are simple macramé knots effective in everything from wall hangings to scarves. When you learn square knots, you'll be ready to spice up your creations with beading. Using crosswise half-hitched knots will bring various designs to your job.

Preparation of The Workspace and Selecting Materials
Determine the rope form that you require, depending on the project.
As there're a lot of rope styles that you may utilize on macramé. You may use cotton thread, string, twine, cloth, or something else that arrives with a chain that is readily pliable.

If you're making jewelry, leather is perfect. Cotton rope fits great while you're hanging aboard, so you can create a sweater or blanket using wool.

Gather some sewing sticks. You may require nails to keep the material of knotting outlying, depending on the knots you'll be making. Stitching nails is a perfect choice for that. You should use thumbtacks, as well.

Establish a committee for the initiative. This need not be something special, just something lightweight, but flexible enough to move through nails. An ancient foam sleeping pad or a garden kneeling pad can be taped to the clipboard. Styrofoam or Balsa wood can also be used.

Select an anchor. The anchor can be the portion of wood, plastic, or metal to which the knotting material is tied. You are going to move it to the head of the project panel and utilize it to expand on it. Relying on the mission, the anchors will variate. If you are making keychain or jewelry, it is definitely safer to get a keyring. A rope or dowel would fit perfectly for bigger tasks.

Beginning the project together with the Head Knot Fold string in half by a Reverse Lark.

You're going to need to double-check the fold is precisely half that. You're going to use the majority of this rope for certainties, so if it's rough, it might impact the majority of the project.

Position the anchor curl underneath. Put the curl created by folding rope in half underneath the rod or dowel with two rope ends above. Put the curl underneath one edge of the ring if you are using a chain, and the curl is centered.

Pull up the string, then down the strings. Drag the curl over the nail, dowel, or ring lip. Paste the finger into the curl to grab all chord halves. Take them down by the rope. The rope and ropes would have the form of a pretzel.

Step back on the string to secure the knot. Keep one hand to carry the nail, dowel, or chain. Let off on two halves of the rope on the other. When you do that, the rope will draw the knot closely against the thread, dowel, or chain.

For new ventures, create several ropes. Many macramé designs would involve a total of two groups of knotting ropes. Therefore, you will require to bind a minimum two head knots of the reverse lark, with two parts of macramé rope on the identical anchor to begin any project.

Development of The Half Knot Pattern

Tie the head knots of a reverse lark next to the anchor. You will attach it closer to the center of the anchor and the rope, ring, or dowel that you use to launch your project.

Differentiate from the knotting ropes and knot-carrying strings. After you have added the head knot of your reverse lark, you should have two ropes dangling off. The knotting rope is the rope to create the knot that you should travel away. Knot-carrying rope may be one that you'll fold under or over the knotting rope to create the knot.

Fold onto the knot-carrying cable to the correct knotting thread. Start from the ropes to the rim. Take the correct knotting rope and place it onto the ropes that hold the center knot. Then push it underneath the knotting rope at the left.

Below the knot-carrying rope bend left knotting thread. Begin with the correct knotting rope at the equal height as where you started. Move left knotting rope to the right, going through the ropes holding the knot. Then put it onto the knotting rope to the right. Push two ropes close before the tie is drawn securely.

Continue to create partial knots to shape a spiral pattern. When you bind more partial knots to the string, there would inevitably be a curl in the rope. How much knots it needs to form one spiral swirl depends on how much heavy your rope is. If you have some of the swirls that you want, pull the rope together.

Build squared knot from the opposite side, by creating a second partial knot. Until the first partial knot has been made, start at the opposing side of the ropes. Bring left knotting rope onto the middle onto knot-carrying strings, push it underneath the correct knotting rope. Then draw the correct knotting rope underneath the ropes that hold the knot and onto the wrong knotting string. Pull the rope to make the knot close and stable.

Having an Opposing Squared Knot design

Bind off a minimum of eight ropes with the head knot of the reverse lark. Make sure that when you bind each rope to your dowel or rod, it's bundled up opposite to the next one.

Divide the cables into four sets. Every combination of four strands creates one knot in a square. If you hooked up your dowel or rod with more than eight strings, that's perfect. You only need to get sufficiently workable ropes to be equally separated by four.

Create one squared knot with four ropes each. Make one squared knot for every four sets of ropes using the procedure mentioned in phase 6 of method 3. You will start with every squared knot from dowel or rod at around the same point so that the squared knots are also horizontal.

Place the next series of knots on line. Where the next series of squared knots begin is on you. In case you require a more compact design (best for scarves or blankets), consider the next row just under the first line. If you want further clarification, lacier design, drop one in (2.5 cm).

Drop on each end of two strings. Leave two ropes on each end of a rope, or dowel free, for next set of squared knots. Then split the sum of ropes leftover by four. That is how much-squared knots you are getting in the next section.

Again, render one squared knot on every four-rope package. Make sure any squared knot begins the same length against the knot before it. This holds an even look on your template.

Attempt to keep two ropes free on each end before ropes wear out. When you have reached the stage that you can no longer equally cut your ropes into four, continue the cycle with all of the sixteen or more ropes that you started with. Then continue as deep down the alternating line as you would like.

Binding a Crosswise Half Hitch

Bind four ropes of reverse lark's head ties. The crosswise half hitch needs one knotting rope and seven knot-carrying ropes. As you'll require to attach four ropes with the reverse lark's knots to have the eight ropes you require. They will be linked really near to each one rod or dowel that you are utilizing.

Determine where the knotting rope would be. You can start from either the left or right-hand side of this design. If you begin on the bottom, the very bottom outside rope will be the knotting rope, and the others will be the knot-carrying ropes. If you start on the right, the very right outside rope will be the knotting rope, and the others are the knot-carrying ropes.

Place the knotting rope to the left side of knot-carrying ropes. A little nail, which you would be utilizing for sewing, can work very well for this. Place a nail in the project panel close to the anchor and simply to the left of the ropes. Pick the knotting rope out and over the nail, then pass over the knot-carrying ropes at a crosswise angle. Seal the edge of the knotting rope with another nail, approximately one in 2.5 cm away from where the first bolt is. In case you require a more impressive crosswise angle, nail the edge of the knotting rope farther away.

Create the first spiral with knotting rope. Thread the knotting rope around the first knot-carrying thread. And drawback the knotting rope under itself. The knotting rope is then curled back onto the first knot-carrying rope. The first moment it's knotted, pull the rope through the curl formed.

Repeat for any chord that knots. When you've twice curled the identical knot-carrying rope, switch on to next knot-carrying rope. Curl the knotting rope twice, the second time you pull the rope into the hole produced by the first curl. Start pulling the ropes close to protect them. Repeat this before the diagonal limit is hit.

Create a twisty design by binding another half-hitch in crosswise. When you meet the diagonal edge, you can create a twisty design by adding a half-hitch diagonally in the opposing direction. Hence this time, if you began to begin on the left side, begin on the right side. Your outer right rope is the knot-binding rope, and all the other ropes to the left side are knot-carrying ropes.

• You should only keep doing the half-hitch diagonally from the identical hand to bring the ties tightly together.

Beads Adding by Utilizing a Knot

Begin by binding a knot (squared). You will require a minimum of one knot (squared) on top of your bead. Tie a knot in a square like you would ordinarily. You may bind on the bead multiple times, but you require a minimum one.

• If you have the bead in the project that doesn't have square ties, that s perfect. Only make sure you have a knot around where the bead is heading.

Slide the ropes that hold the knot through the ring. These two ropes in the middle you use in forming a squared knot, and you will move the bead up till the knot over it is bundled with.

Bind a knot (squared) to the bead when the bead is bundled with the squared knot over it by utilizing the knotting ropes to form a squared knot beneath. Squared knot beneath that you bind will also be bundled with the bead's edge.

Repeat for any number of beads you want. You may construct a design of a lot of knots (squared), with the beads, or simply utilizing a single bead to complete the project.

How can you choose the right fiber for your project?

Selecting the correct fiber is an essential first phase before beginning a new project. This can be a really enjoyable and exciting experience because there are so many choices, but if you don't know where to proceed, it can also be a little daunting. So, let's just break it down a little.

fiber Content:

If you're searching for thread, chain, string, or yarn, you'll want to determine whether to use a NATURAL or SYNTHETIC fiber to deal with.

Natural fabrics include cotton, linen, jute, wool, and hemp, and they are suitable for indoor crafts, home design, shoes, clothing, gift wrap, and textiles. They are also biodegradable, so they are a good earth-friendly crafting choice.

Synthetic fabrics contain polypropylene, acrylic, nylon & rubber, which are suitable for outdoor ventures because they can withstand rain or sun well and do not break down with the weather over time.

Size:

The rope comes in such a large range of sizes/diameters, others being more appropriate than others for other tasks.

Smaller Strings, 3 mm or less fit well for jewelry, as well as small or fragile designs. Medium Ropes, 4mm-7 mm, is the more widely used, a better size for macramé learners, sturdier than the smaller ropes, and the best size for plant hangers, wall hangings, chairs, lanterns, curtains, rugs, etc. Wide Ropes, 8mm-12 mm (and bigger) give a dramatic statement and are so enjoyable to work with, particularly for wall hangings. Because of their scale, they may be a little more difficult to deal with but worth the effort.

Texture:

The texture is an essential factor to remember creatively because the addition of a nice fiber with texture will definitely bring value to a product. You might also want to know how the fiber feels to deal with, particularly if you're knotting up anything large-a fiber-like jute looks great but, on the hands, can be a bit rough. But, luckily not to fear, gloves are a good way to save your hands while dealing with a rugged textured material.

COTTON is easy to deal with and so flexible it can be used for almost any project. It's simple on the neck, gentle to the touch, and it comes in several sizes and textures. We sell Cotton Rope & String, and all our cotton is 100 percent Oeko Tex Certified manufactured by our Turkish maker specifically for Modern Macramé.

Cotton Rope is available in 5 mm 3-ply (what we use with all our workshops and what we prefer with beginners), 12 mm 3-ply (for your large-scale or heavy projects), and 3 mm 2-ply (this rope fits good for smaller, smoother, more fragile projects).
Our Cotton String is extremely smooth, perfectly ties together and almost effortless, and is available in 2 mm 1-ply, 4 mm 1-ply, and 9 mm 1-ply.

JUTE is a durable, natural fiber of lovely grain and color. It is rough and scratchy, but it is a strong practical fiber that looks perfectly knotted.
Jute Rope comes with a 1-ply 6 mm.

FELTED WOOL is a nice, soft, and voluminous statement fiber. Using it to create a lush and elegant pillow, or give some wooly decoration to a hanging rope board.
The Felted Wool is provided in 1-ply, approx.10-12 mm.

POLYPROPYLENE is a long-lasting, strong rope and will perform up in the weather, making it a popular option for outdoor projects.

Polypropylene Rope comes in braided 6 mm.

Chapter 3 Macramé knots

The simple knots below for having you off. With only those simple ties under your belt, you can do so many things. Keychains, bookmarks, placemats, bracelets with macramé, wall hangings with macramé twist, plant and pot hangers, etc. I like cording. But Amazon does have Lots of decent macramé cording choices. And don't mention you can even have all manner of colors. Study the comments to figure out what will best for you.

Then, we will have a circle, a handle, or a chain. Only to tie the cable to anything like this.

Lark's head macramé knot

The lark head-knot is the best way to begin every macramé design. They should be faced in front or back. Here's how to make both of it.

The head ties of the front-facing lark by putting a line of cord sitting until wrapped against the dowel.

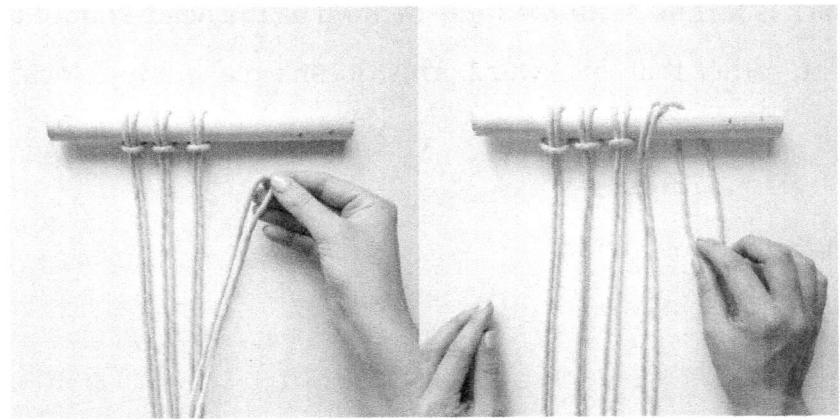

1. For your project, weigh and split a cord wide.

2. Align both ends and split the string in two.

3. Functioning from the front side, on the top of dowel taking the folded loop, then drop behind it, with the loop pointing downwards.

4. 4. Pull up and through the loop on the two split tails of the rope, then twist to seal your knot.

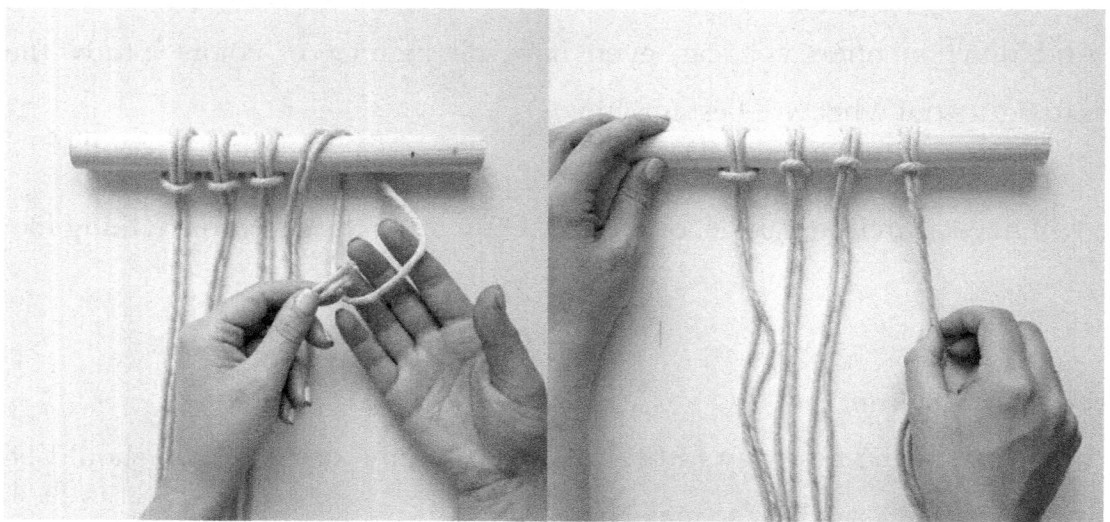

(Reverse lark's head) macramé knot

The head-knot of a reverse lark is formed with the same method as the head-knot of a lark, only moving against you rather than backward. This doesn't make any "block" noticeable on your dowel.

1. For your project, weigh and split a cord wide.

2. Align both ends and split the string in two.

3. Put the folded curve on the dowel's top, operate from the rear, then downward in forwarding of it, with the loop face forward.

4. Pull up and through the loop, the two split ends of the thread, then twist to close your knot of reverse lark's head.

Wrap macramé knot

This is a knot that is used at the start or last of a macramé item to secure groups of cords.

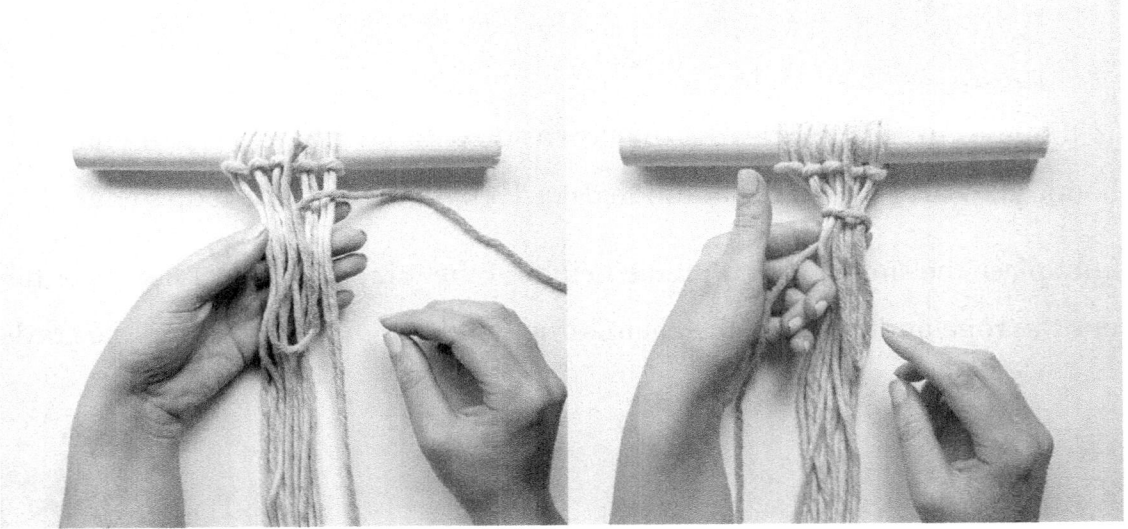

1. Measure and split a long thread.

2. Collect the cords in your left side hand that you want to fasten as a line. Build a down faced circle with the cord end, leaving a small tail and the left behind cord end at the upper right.

3. Pinch the left thumb and index finger on top and tail of the loop. Use the diameter of the cord beneath the group and move it back to the left to build one loop, and tie it around.

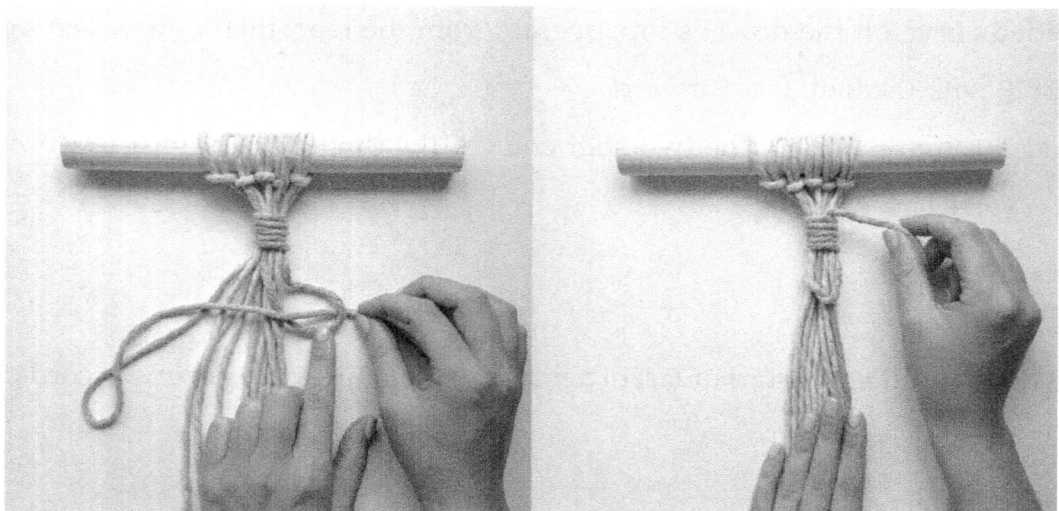

4. Assure that the curve is left clear at the downside before wrapping when you have tightly bound the party thread the additional cord length through the loop's edge.

5. Carefully place the small tail end on the height of the wraps to protect the cover tie. It shortens the rope and captures the chain, dragging it upwards back onto the cords tied.

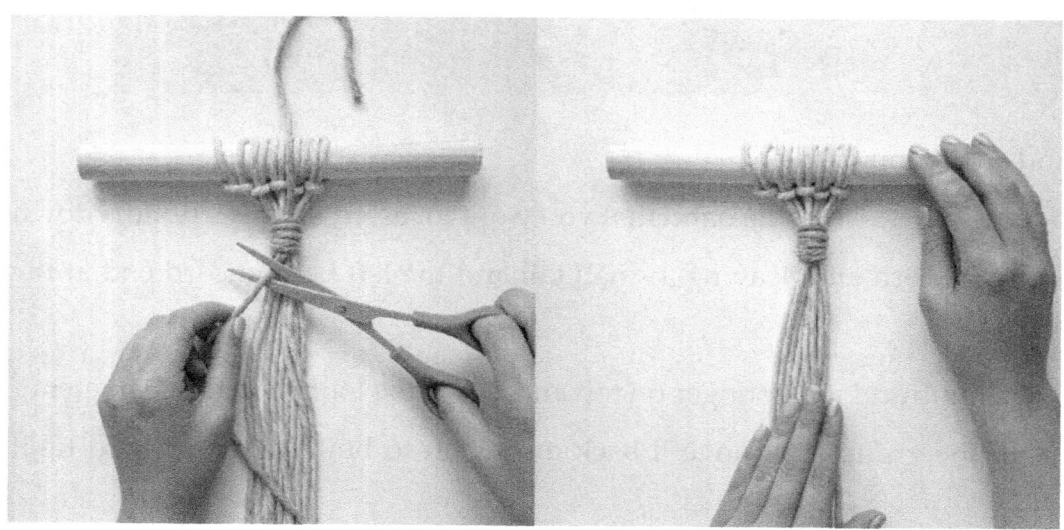

6. Eliminate the remaining length and tail to get neaten at the bottom and top of the wrap. Full Tie macramé tie.

Half hitch macramé knot

These knots are basically used to attach support on a slice of macramé.

1. Select the cord pairs to which you want to bind a half hitch of macramé knot.

2. Taking the tails of the pair of cords to the right side of the static cords or draw them down and forward, forming a circle or form D.

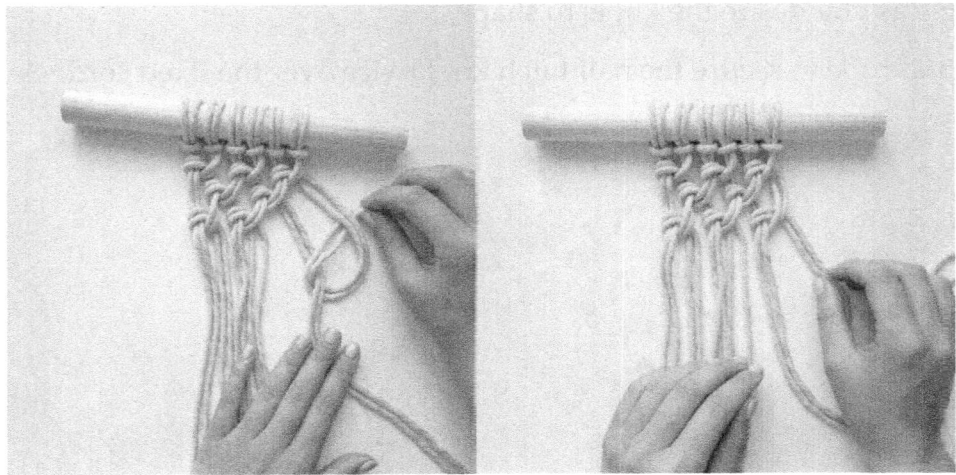

3. Grab the tails of D cords, overlap them at the place of rest where these cords actually meet, then connect them through the D string.

4. Pull softly in the desired place to hold.

A pair of half hitch macramé knot

It is also classified as a double hitch knot, which is a half hitch type, where the cycle is replicated twice. It is also used in macramé bits to build vertical and horizontal patterns or to introduce different colors.

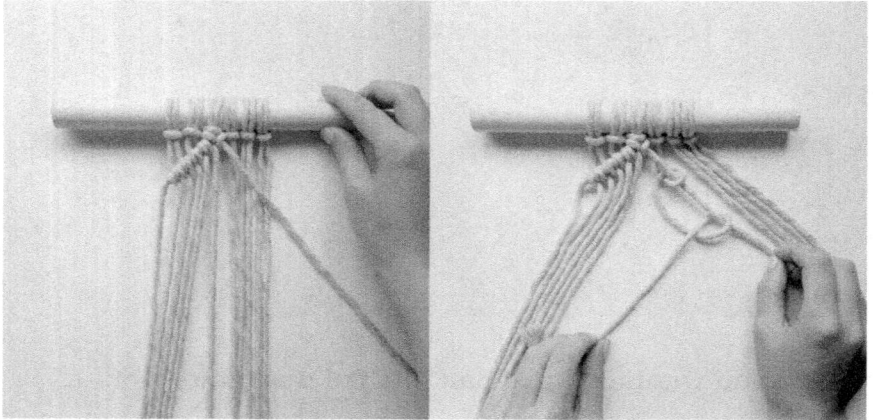

1. To attach a double half hook around, use a fixed cord. Keep the static cord at the appropriate line angle as you desire the knots to shape.

2. Using the right-hand rope to secure the half hitch knot twice over the fixed cord.

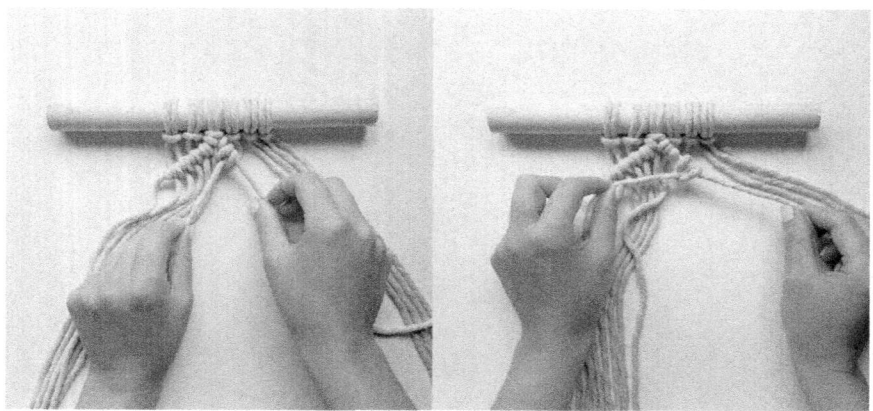

3. To secure the ties, remove the covered cord, and then shift them to the required location when keeping the fixed string at the required angle.

4. By Using the next static string, repeat measures 1-3.

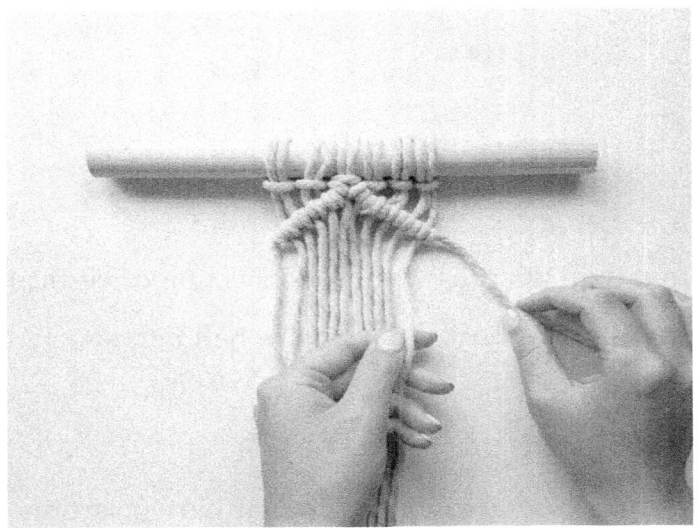

5. Repeat Measures 1-4 to finish a double half hitch diagonal line.

Horizontal double half hitch macramé knots

Horizontal double half-hitch knots are perfect for adding new colors to an object or to create a straight-line appearance of a line of horizontal knots. These are also used in wall hangings created by macramé.

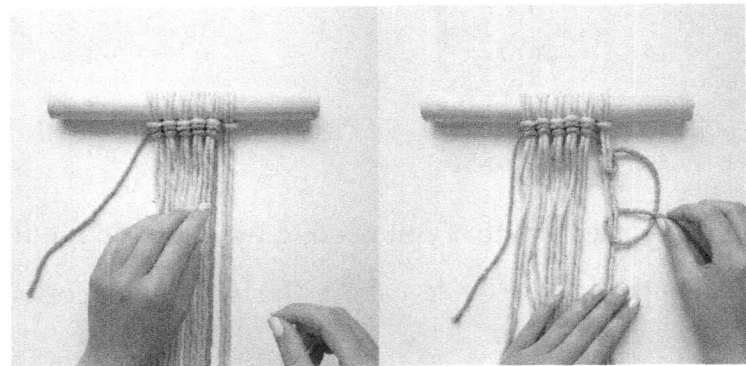

1. A colored rope is weighed and split in half.

2. Take a set of static strings, and using the colored rope to tie through two half-hitch macramé knots.

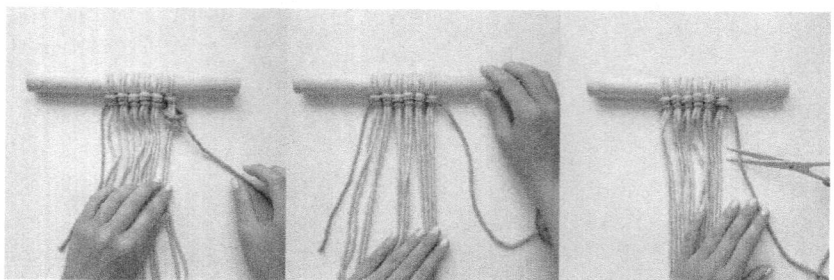

3. Not like the angled dual half hitch knot, you will pick the next collection of vertical fixed cords to tie the follow-on ties to each step for horizontal double half hitches.

4. Cut the tails of the strings left over.

How to make a square macramé knot

These knots are quick, durable, and flexible. It is necessary to do that in two sections while making a square type macramé knot, binding the knot's first-half working towards left and the remaining half of the knot operating to the right.

How to fix a knot in square-part 1

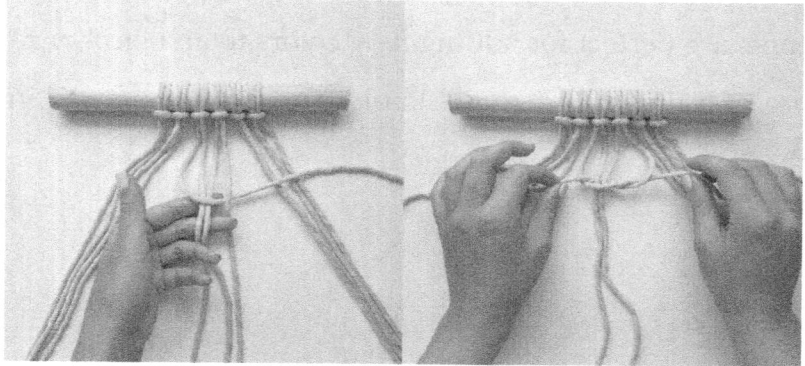

1. To build the square knot, pick the two cord pairs that you need to work on. To build a backward D-shaped coil, take the tail of the cord to the left above the two Center cords and below the right-hand cord.

2. Take the tail of right-hand chord and move across the D-shaped backward, through the two cords in the Middle and above the left-hand string.

How to fix a knot in a square – Part 2

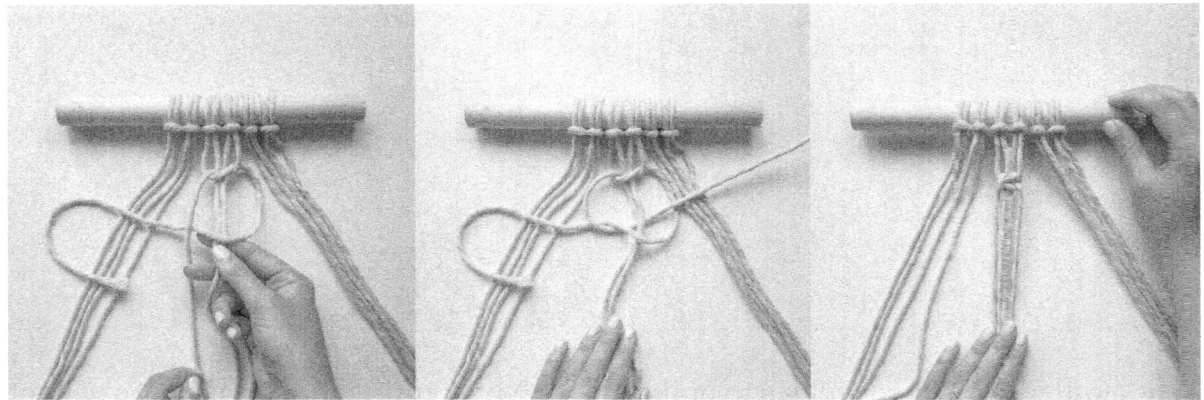

3. Repeat Steps 1-2 to complete the knot square, this period mirroring the behavior by dealing on the wrong cord sides. So, as Step 1, build a D form with your right chord, moving over the cords in the middle and below the chord in the west.

4. Take the cord on the left and stretch it into the D formation, under the cords in the middle and above the cord on the right. Squeeze the strings to close. Then done! Total Macramé Tie.

Alternation of the square macramé knots?

A flexible and decorative strategy can be to rotate the positioning of square macramé knots inside hanging cord sets. It is also used for the formation of geometric shapes, including diamonds and triangles.

1. Work underneath knot squares to build a new chain, putting the early square of knot among the knots on the top. To do so, connect the current square knot utilizing the square knot's the two right: hand cords on top, and the knot's two left-hand cords above and towards the side.

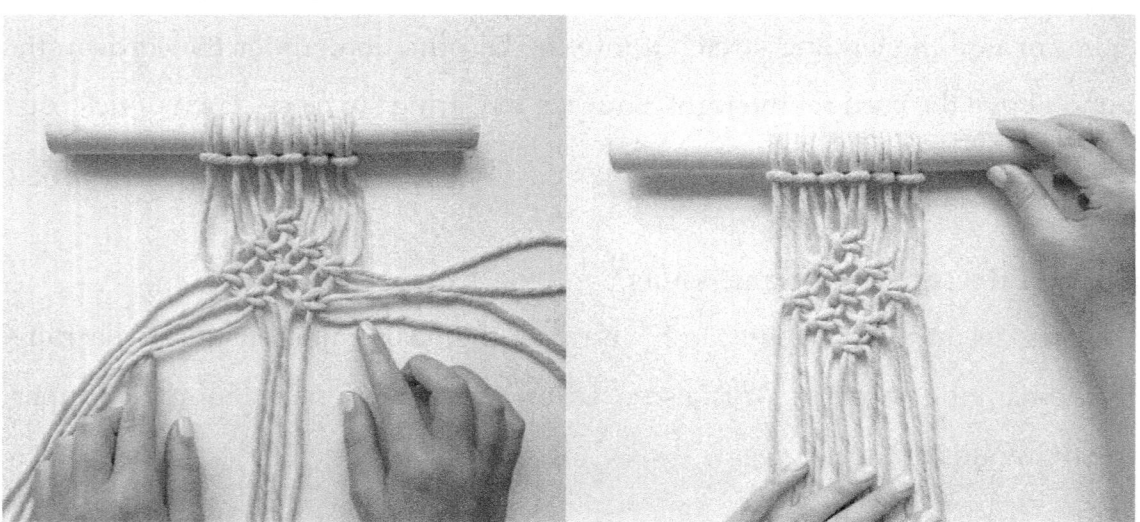

2. You will always choose a pair of right-hand or left-hand cords from one knot in an above row, and the opposing combination from a knot ahead to it, to proceed to tie square knots in an alternating fashion.

Half-square Spiral Knot

They also called as helix knots, the spirals of the half square, are simple to create, solid and decorative.

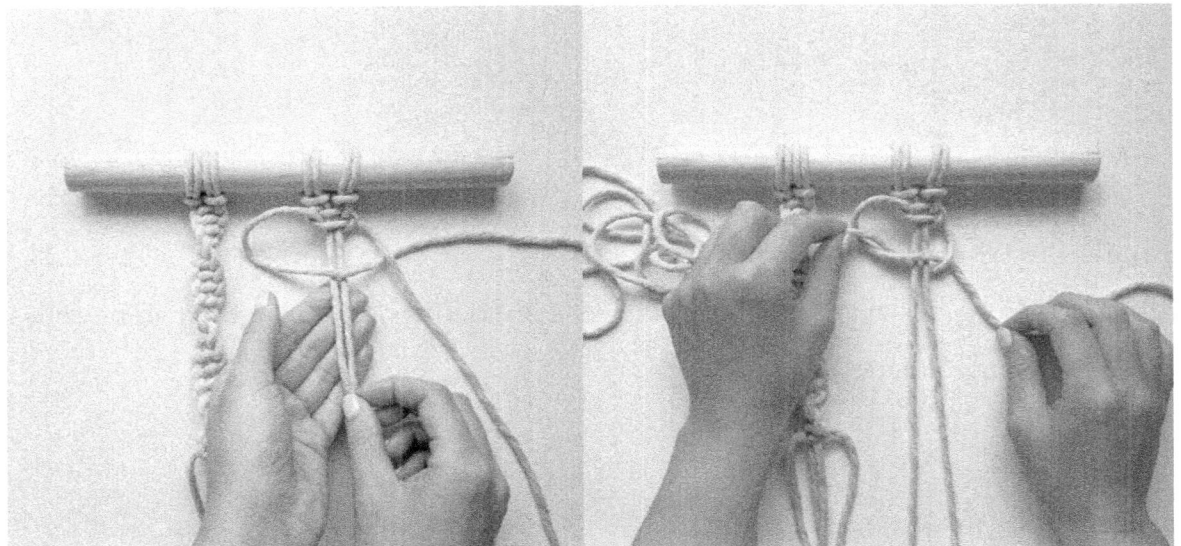

1 Attach step 1 of a knotted square, pick the two cord pairs you choose to use, and take the left cord above the two Middle cords and below the right cord to make a D-shaped curve backward. First, take the right-hand tail of the chord and move it into the D-shaped backward, passing through the two cords in the Middle and above the left string.

2 Not like the square knot, you don't need to duplicate or switch the sides that you're focused on to proceed to build a series of knots. Do Phase 1 several times, instead. The macramé knots, of course, continue spiraling.

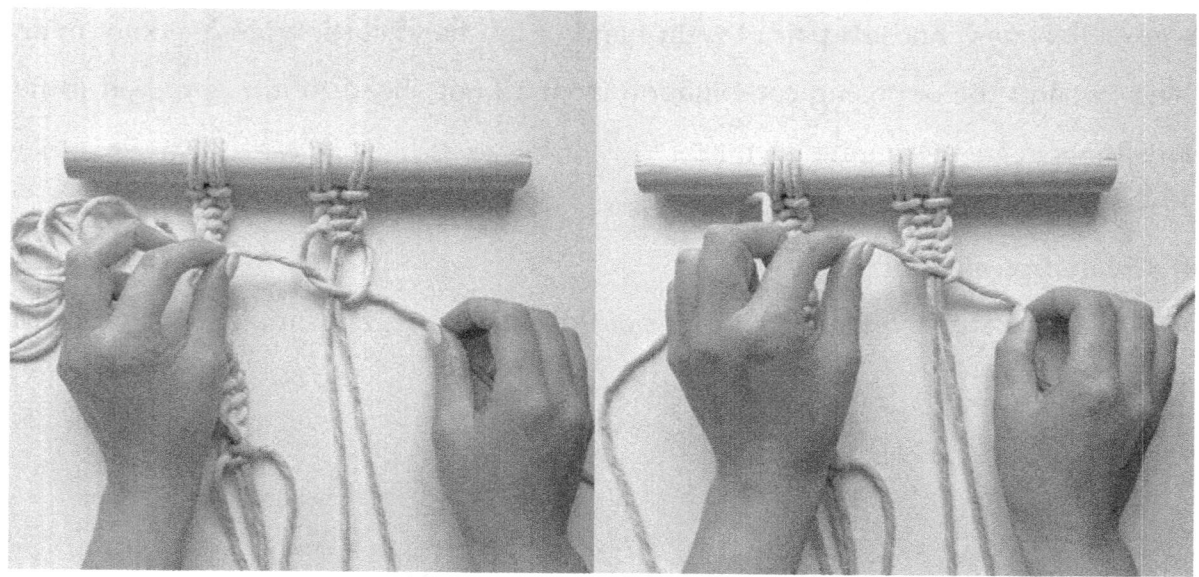

How to fix the fringes?

Textured fringing gives every macramé project a boho look. Your fringe finishing relies on the chord you are using.

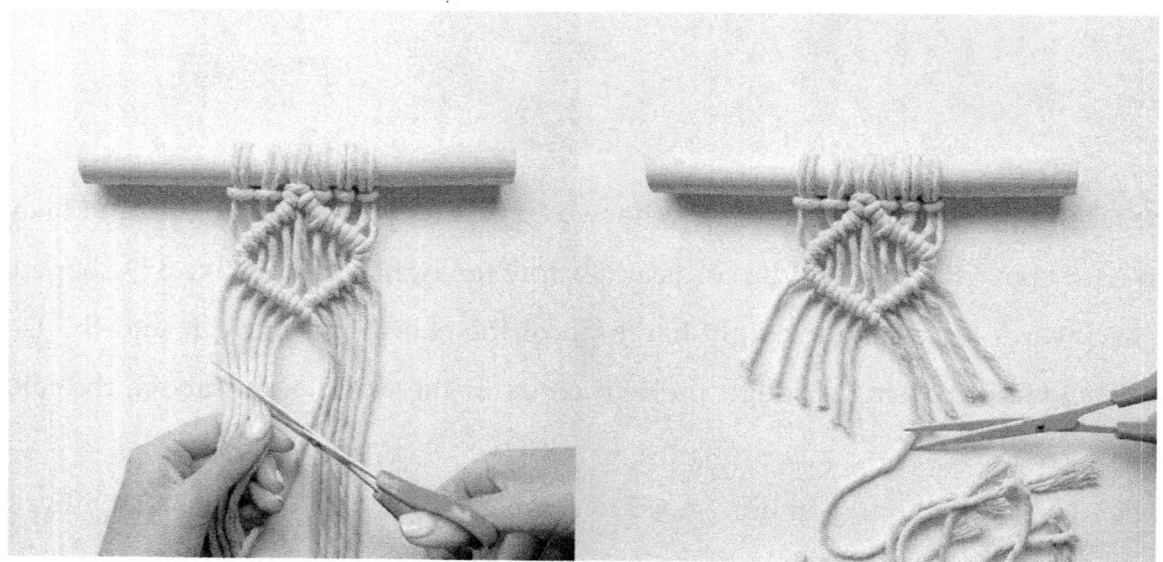

1. Cut the hanging cords remaining lengths to the required amount.

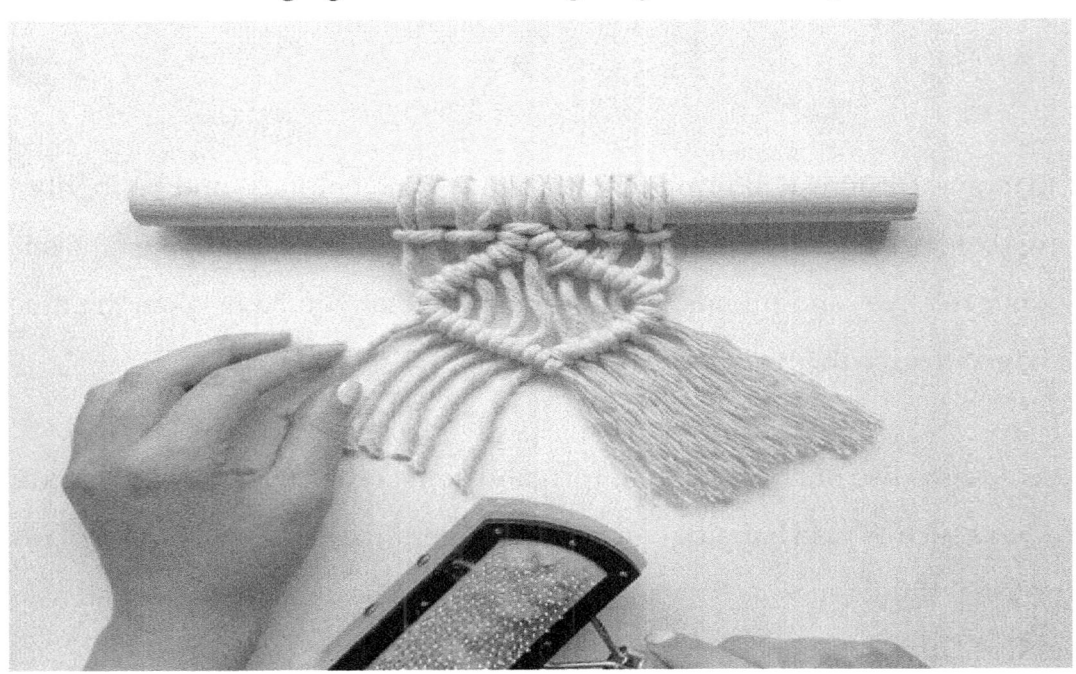

2. Next, using a hard brush, brush them carefully to distinguish them, start at the tails and progressively work up.

3. Finally, depending on the preferred finish, cut the edges in a vertical way or into the circle.

Chapter 4: Macramé patterns

Some macramé designs will bring to your home some boldness and boho vibes and are cost-friendly enough to create many of them! They even make fantastic gifts; your relatives and friends would appreciate that you have taken the time of your own hands to give them all special.

Many of these designs use only a macramé cord and some other materials. Of typical macramé products such as wall hangings and plant hangers, there are macramé designs and certain unusual things such as keychains, trivets, curtains, table runners, and also chandeliers and chairs.

Macramé Mason basin Plant Hanger

Here's another variant to put on a macramé plant hanger. Each one is clearly designed to accommodate a canning or mason pot. To complete this project, the thing you need is a basin, some macramé wire, and scissors.

Macramé Plant Hanger

Make a classic plant hanger for macramé, which you can hang inside or out. This is a classic style that also uses a cord of its own to build the rope it should hang on.

Macramé Laptop Mat

Here's a macramé template for the laptop mats, which might be utilized for a placemat, small table runner, or maybe a trivet as well. To build an elaborate pattern, it utilizes the cube, diagonal 1/2 hitch, and horizontal 1/2 hitch knots.

Macramé Wall Hanging

Macramé wall hangings are a common method to showcase your knotting abilities, and this design and demonstration offer you step-by-step instructions on how to hang this wall using just a few simple knots to build it.

Giant Macramé Rope Lights

Create a sign with this big rope light macramé. It'll bring an element of mystery to every space in your house! To create this exclusive piece of macramé, you will require cording, including a lamp cord and plug package.

Dyed Macramé Necklace

You can create this beautiful macramé necklace with leather stitching, some thread, and dye for fabric. Modify this fast evening project by adjusting the dye's color or keeping it undented for a complete boho feel.

Macramé Top

Take a t-shirt, and you'll have a macramé cover with a couple of snips and ties. This one shows a painted white t-shirt, but you might use every t-shirt in your wardrobe to build a trendy feel.

Scandinavian Knotted trivet:

Bring a bit of Scandinavian style to your sitting room or kitchen, use this We Are Scout macramé trivet template. A handmade embroidery hoop with a few beads creates this trivet a cost-friendly, style-free creation.

Macramé Earrings

Take a hoop earring and also a macramé cord, and both of you are able to make these awesome earrings. The instructions are incredibly simple to obey, and in less than an hour, you can have a fresh pair of earrings to yourself.

Macramé Feather Wall Decorations

Build a wall show that will inspire your mates over giant feathers with this macramé design. You might quickly adjust the design to make feathers smaller, which would be perfect for keyrings or even decorations.

Macramé Dream Catcher

Simply naming this, a dream catcher may not add justice to it. This beautiful hanging wall will look amazing in a school, bedroom, or elsewhere in your house.

Macramé Curtain

This macramé curtain should offer some space, some anonymity, as well as a lot of styles if you need a bedroom divider or a wardrobe cover.

Hanging Macramé Chair

You can make a hanging macramé seat with the plastic seat frame and plenty of patience that seems like it comes right from a high-end shop. This guide contains several mistakes and failures to help you make it a success.

Macramé Table Runner

Bring a piece of comfort and design to your living room with this The DIY Mommy macramé table runner. This table runner, influenced by one at Anthropologie, will offer you the chic boho look that anyone would envy.

Boho Macramé Wall Hanging

Here is the bohemian-design macramé wall hanging template that uses only four knots to make an amazing looking, relatively basic design. It is such a flexible template; you're going to want to create it for all you meet.

Macramé Chandelier

Here's another statement piece of macramé — this time in the shape of a chandelier. Cording and even a lampshade will build the jaw-dropping chandelier, which will take you to complete a good part of the day.

Macramé Bracelets

This macramé bracelet lesson packs quite the punch though simpler than the other macramé designs. To make these trendy bracelets, using jewelry string and connectors.

Macramé Bookmark

This macramé template is for a bookmark that looks amazing, sitting among books on your coffee table. It's a fast piece to make, and for any occasion, it would be a great gift too.

Macramé Garden Chair

Here is another macramé chair template except this one uses a lawn chair frame and various cord shades to give it a sleek twist retro look.

Chapter 5: Indoor project ideas

There's an infinite range of ways to practice a new talent or art, much like everything in existence. I'm not going to pretend I'm a macramé specialist. I'm a complete newbie, really. I'm actually going to guide you on my unique experience from one beginner to another and teach you one way to do things.

I'll provide you with all the tools you need to make your own way to enjoy the cool macramé art. The best thing is you don't need to be a specialist in making beautifully stunning items of furniture for your house. Honestly, it looks a lot harder than it is. Let's get to it, then.

Retro styles to show macramé in house.

A Trend from the past to the blast

Macramé has seen its flash in the fame through many times of history. When many people imagine such twisted bits of art, they always look back to the time when it hit the highest point of joy — the seventies, when the craze became all -bohemian-things.

Yet its success predated hundreds of years until the age of grooviness and bell-bottoms. It was initially of all the fashion of Arab Weavers of the 13th century. In the 17th century, Queen Mary applied this to the UK. Later, in the Victorian period, the weaving method saw another resurgence, emerging as simple, knotted patterns on lacy designs, nearly 100 years until it appeared again in the 1970s.

And now it's again back, and maybe due to creative artisans and designers, it's better than ever. When the patterns in decoration move to boho specifics and quirky style, there has been a gradual evolution to taking back macramé.

If you haven't hopped aboard the new-day macramé ship, you might picture the crumbling owl with descend eyes hanging for decades in the corner of the house of your mother. Although those macramé items can actually be right in vintage-inspired spaces, fresh, today's patterns marry the new and the old, using inventively old ideas.

In order to stay faithful to the previous essence of macramé, although adopting them in the 21st century, below are few inspirations for the designs to get you going.

Fiber Art

When viewed as a futuristic interpretation of the dreamcatcher, Macramé's artwork gives a change into current times. Hoops and soft macramé create works of art ideal for the daily. Dreamcatchers are usually placed over the bunk, a place where items like this will feel right at home.

Plant Hangers

It gets no more classic macramé than a hanger to a tomato. There's no denying that your mom had some sort of hanging in your house as you grew up. Now those plants are trendy again, and also leafy greens cover on-trend location, macramé plant hangers give any sense, particularly those hangers with twisted, subtle detailing. For the perfect Instagram-ready setting, hang yours along with walls.

Wall Hangings

The wall hangings appear to be the norm when it's about macramé. Do you choose lightweight or strong weaving? Long or short? Dip-dyed or white? And nowadays, only macramé wall art can be ordered that suspended from a recycled part of driftwood. They are flexible and can suit virtually everywhere in the house, including a pint-sized wall that requires anything to cover it or a room where it could be contrasted with framed photos.

Votive Holders

How's that creative? Small glass jars dressing up to make their own macramé. The weavings give to the candle holders a touch of coziness, where they can be viewed on a nightstand, a bath counter, or even an outdoor patio.

Patterned Stools

Macramé often makes a beautiful addition to a bench or chair, each of two as a decorative decoration, or as a nice place to relax, whether the yarns are durable. Be that as it might, it may look cute placed in a corner between decorative items and plant, or show many over a dining table.

Woven Hammocks

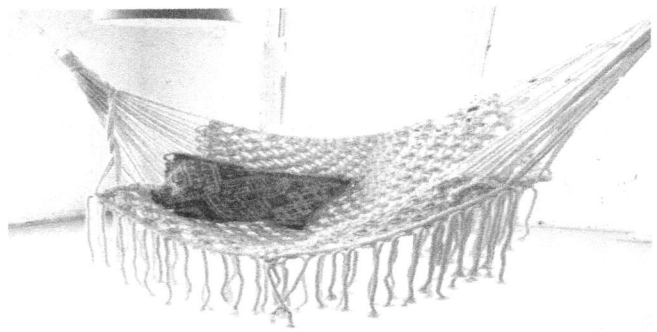

Yeah, in a backyard will be the throwback place to view a macramé hammock, but we think it fits much better inside. Hang it in a corner to act as a laid-back reading nook or on a three-season porch where you can enjoy Netflix and soak in the outdoor scenery.

Knit Placemats

Making your house appear as if by showing macramé placemats or a runner on your dining room table, it sprang from the pages of an Anthropologie catalog. Macramé functions for a wide range of tablescapes, from boho to beach and most of all. It conveys a calm and modeled environment.

Decorative Garlands

It is no accident that a macramé garland might possibly act as a belt might have been carried by Stevie Nicks in the '70s. Alternatively, place yours at this, above your bed or fence, or around a windowsill, on such a wall hanger.

Door Curtains

This isn't almost as loud as the string curtains of the 70s. Hang a floating macramé curtain for a touch of dreaminess to attach to every doorway.

Hanging Chandeliers

Bring a chandelier made in macramé into your decor for a glimpse of a flower-child. You may either hang it as a discussion piece of its own, or others have the option to bring an LED light into the room, projecting a magical glow throughout. Yeah, macramé is shion theme, so we don't know how long it's going to hang around

enjoy it while here.

ic Coil Bowl

a neon flash with those woven coil bowls to your desk or shelves. They will also

ake a beautiful homemade present, maybe a small bowl with a few washi tapes rolls

inside? ... Not much until Christmas.

What YOU will NEED:

Long fabric strips – everything will work: I used both cotton and acrylic knits. The blu neon in a discount bin was the dirt-cheap yard, and the gray lines were Zpagetti thread. You may also use pieces of clothing, recycled T-shirts, or thrifted fabrics and tablecloths.

Cord – the fluorescent orange from the hardware store is 'Brickie's Side' ($5 per 100 meters) – and you can use more fabric or yarn as I did for the pink cups. You'll use the best of this. For the gray bowl, I used about 8 – 10 meters (about 8.5 – 11 yards), and it s around 14 cm (5.5 inches) long x 8 cm (3.5 inches) thick. The number seen in the picture below is not a true representation.

A large needle in the thread with a wide head.
Scissors.

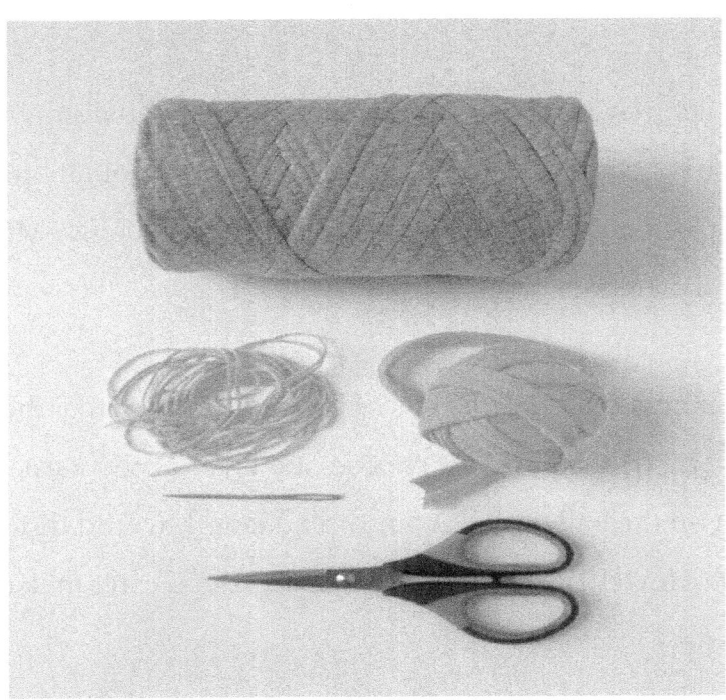

, mats, cotton yard, etc.), the thicker, the chunkier you cut it, and

wl would be. A decent size for tiny bowls is around 3.5 cm (1.5) "long.

n below shows how one piece of fabric may be sliced into a continuous

cut the fabric to extend it at a time in tiny pieces and the fabric coils into a

ortable circular 'yarn' shape.

red lines indicate cuts

The instructional pictures are of neon orange stitching for the gray pot, so from now on, I'll stick to those shades. Let's continue ... Cut the length of an orange cord as far as you can without it being twisted, then loop it with the needle. Mine was around 2 meters (just below 2 meters).

To get a decent thickness, I used three bits of grey cotton yarn together. I cut it down to around 1.4 meters (4.5 ft) wide. If you choose one layer of the yarn, it doesn't need to be sliced; it may sit on the ball/spool. Your thread length would differ on whether you want to alter colors. However, it's all pretty free style-you can't make errors!

Overlap the orange cord ends and grey yarn as well—four to Five times Loop the string around the thread.

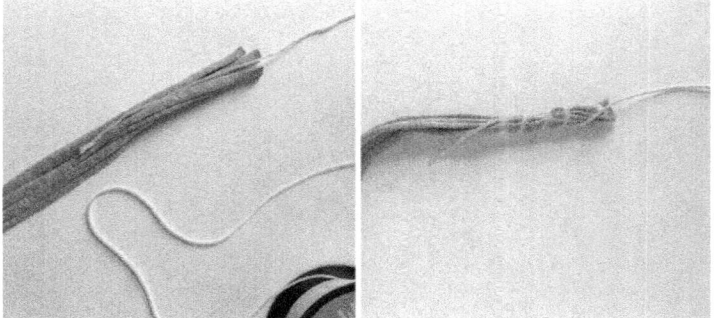

Fold the grey yarn end over to create a circle. Keep the hole as tiny as you can in the middle – it will be only wide enough to go through the needle because it should become wider when you stitch across the yarn. Wrap the cord around the yarn loop center, let a short tail stick out, and tie a knot. (As in the screenshot to the left below). Keep the yarn as seen on top of the short tail and on the bottom of the long piece of yarn. Take the needle around to the back of the loop and move it through you through the hole (right-hand image).

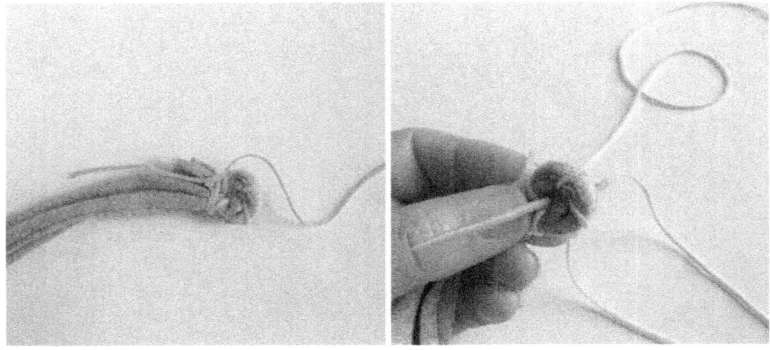

Do not knot the rope-leaving a rope at the top (as seen in the photo below). Then pass through the loop, through the needle, much like a thread on a scarf.

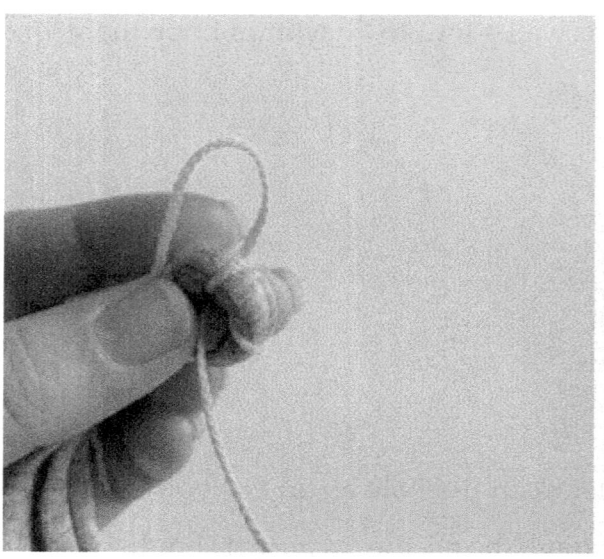
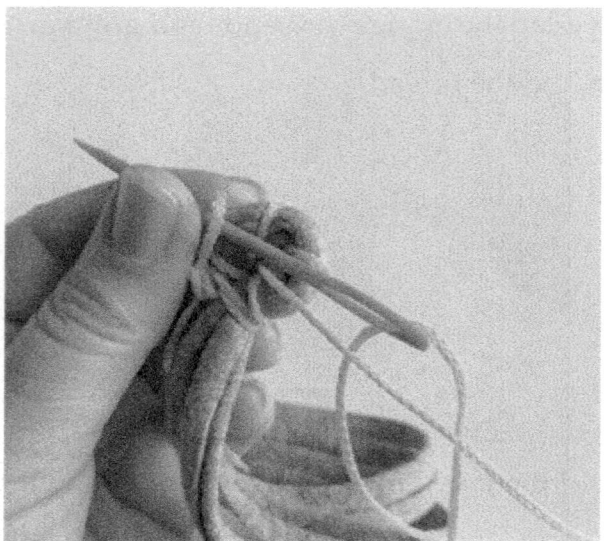

Repeat the stitch around the loop all the way. Needle in from back to front through the opening. Leave a thread, and pass into it the pin. Push closed knot. The stitch should be strong but not heavy. Hold the stitches tight together and move around (like in the picture below on the right hand).

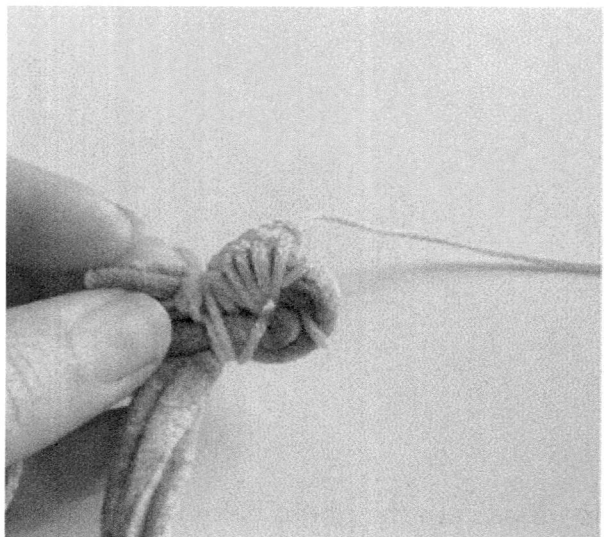

Fold over the orange cord's starting tail and the gray yarn's short tail on top with the long gray yarn (left-hand picture below). Your next stitch would go through your first blanket stitch in the back rather than through the opening. Bring the needle out to the back of the first blanket stitch and put it around the edges. The next stitch passes across the top of the second stitch on the scarf. Move down to the next picture for a closer peek at where the arrow moves.

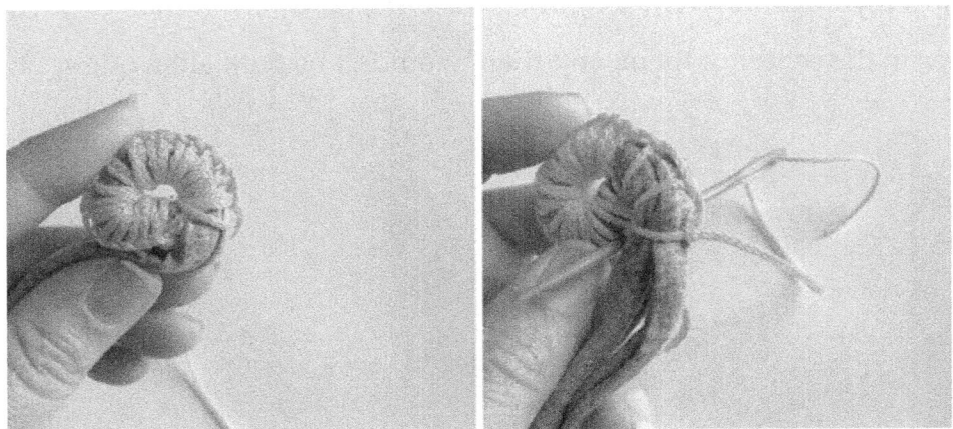

You've done a lot of stitching, and you possibly would quickly run out of thread. The photo below to the right illustrates how to attach a new cord duration. Knot the two parts together, such that the knot is on the coil's edge.

Race the tails over the grey thread and tuck them in with the knot while you start stitching (see image below left). I sometimes inserted an additional stitch when my coil expanded as I felt they were growing too far away. Recall not drawing the stitches so close, so the bowl's foundation won't sit level.

What you have to do is combine the old with the fresh as you run out of colors or decide to swap colors. I cut everyone a different length because I used three strands of yarn and put the fresh ones in the center of them, and there wouldn't be bulk all in one spot.

As the thread of fabric appears to curl up, I open up every piece and put the fresh one into it. So just keep on sewing.

 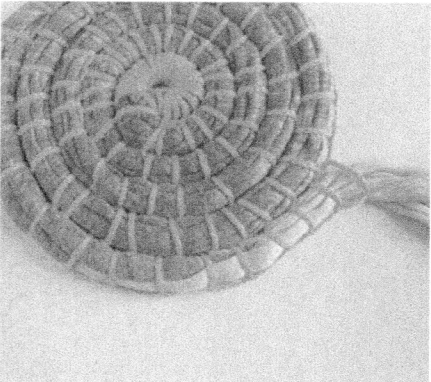

When you are happy with the base size, you will start to build up the sides. Give the stitches a little firmer when keeping the thread above, instead of next to the previous coil. Go on like this until the target height is achieved.

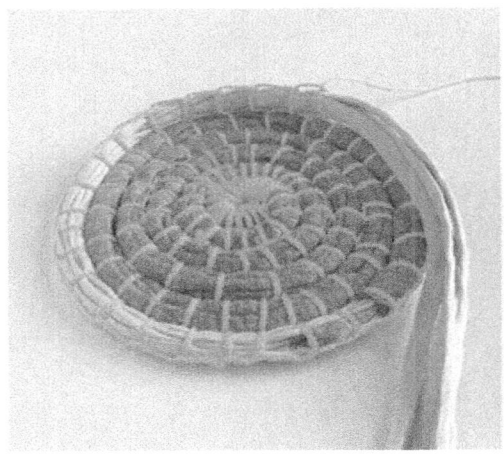 

Moving off. If more than one strand of yarn is used to split them at spaced lengths to reduce the weight, continue to stitch around until there's only one strand remaining. Left on 10 cm (4 inches) of the tail, and you've got ample research to do.

 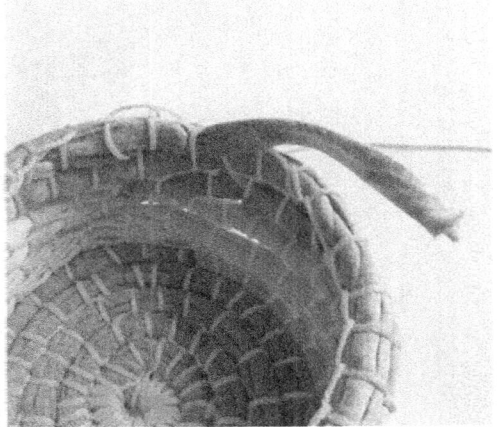

Weave the tails into one of the vertical stitches (on the inside of the bowl) below the lines. Then thread in with a couple more stitches in that row and cut off the yarn, so the tail doesn't stand out (picture below on the left). To finish off the thread, do one more stitch to complete the bowl's top edge, then attach a tiny knot and loop the thread back into the bowl's middle. Break the string, then tuck in the edge.

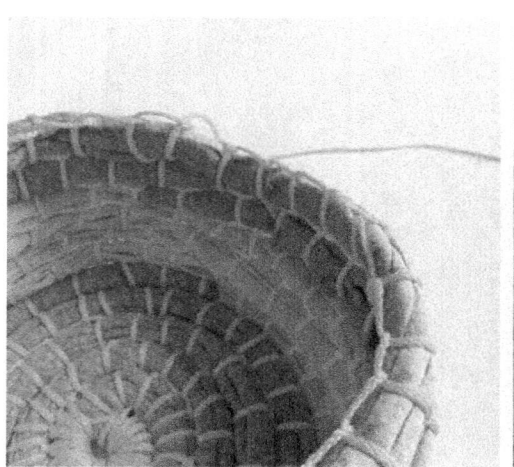 

And done! I consider it really addictive, and now I've created quite a few bowls and baskets in various sizes. Once you get going, it's really very quick. And it's a smart way to do cotton upcycle.

Macramé candle holder

1. You need: thread in cotton, empty container, scissors

2. Break long cord around the container, which you must attach (cord A). I cut cord 40 cm in length for my idea.

3. Split lengthy cables (cord B). Knotting makes the job even shorter, just quick enough to sever the cords. My container has a height of 13 cm. I cut out 56 single cords-45 cm long each. I divided them into two and ended with 112 cords. Remember: You must combine the cords into a set of 4 cords. In this design, every knot is made of 4 cords. I have 112 cords in my house, with 28 groups of four cords.

4. Larks knots in the Back. We must use Larks Knots to fasten all cords B to A one's.

Half Fold cord B and put cord A under it. Pull cord B tails via loop (see picture). Tight pull. Echo on the other B-cords.

5. I attached ends of cord A to 2 keys in my desk drovers to make my job simpler. You may use a chair, for example.

I knotted the head-knot of 56 larks. That brings 112 cords.

6. Knot Square. We'll launch our square knots pattern with sennit. Make a cord A and split ends around the basin. To make a square knot, take (1,2,3,4) four cords: a) put the right one (4th one) towards the left below the two centered cords (2nd & 3rd) and the left cord (1st one). Put the left cord (1) above the two center cords (2,3) to the right, and below the right chord. Pull both the left and right cords (1st and 4th one) to firmly connect the knot.

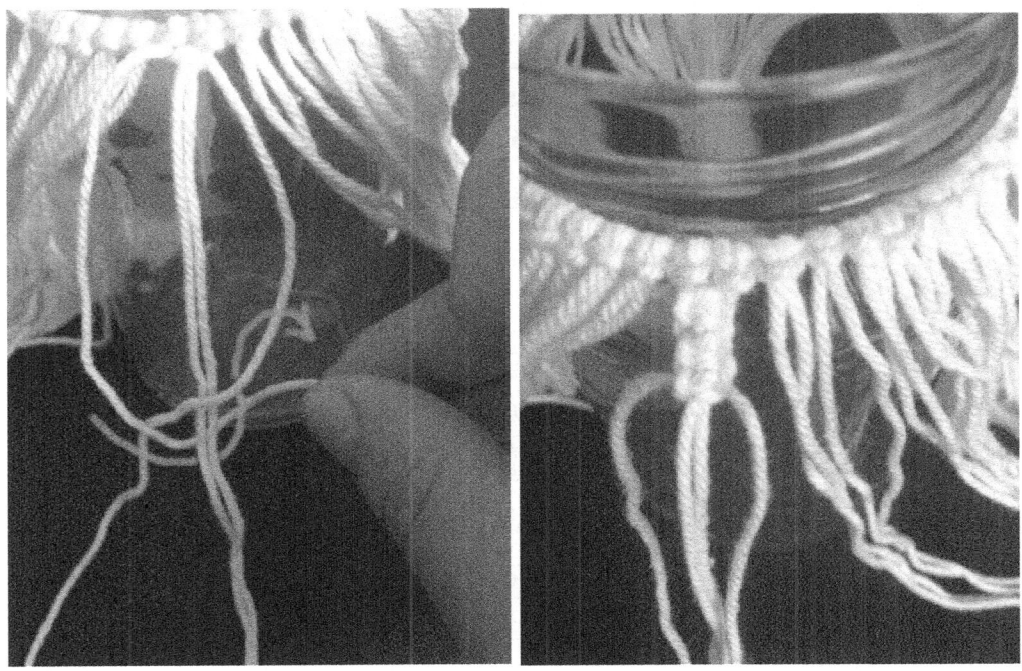

B) Put the right (4th one) cord towards the left above the two center (2,3) cords and below the left (1st) chord. Place the left one below two center cords (2nd & 3rd) to the right, then above the right cord (4th one). Stretch cords right and left to secure your knot (1,2).

7. Make three square knots of sennit on every 4-cord ring. (Sennit-knot links, bound one after the other)

8. Stretch 4. Triangles-ties alternate in line. To make triangles, split the cords into different pairs. To build four reversed triangles, I split my 112 cords by 28. Using the alternative square knots to create a triangle-pick two right strings (3rd & 4th one) from one sennite and two of the left cords (1st & 2nd) from the next sennite and make knot squares.

For my triangle development project, I made: Row four to seven alternative square knots, Row five to six alternative square knots, Row six to five alternative square knots, Row seven to row four alternative square knots, Row eight to 3rd row, alternative square knots, Row nine to row 2nd alternative square knots, Row ten to row 1st alternative square knots. I produced a further three triangles using the same pattern.

Note: If you have a specific amount of cords, you can do some maths. For e.g., you can combine them into 25 4-cord combines if you have 100 cords, and create five triangles (each triangle would have 20 cords= five alternating square knots). You can divide them into 30 4-cord sets if you have 120 cords, and create six triangles (each triangle would have 20 cords = 5 alternating square knots).

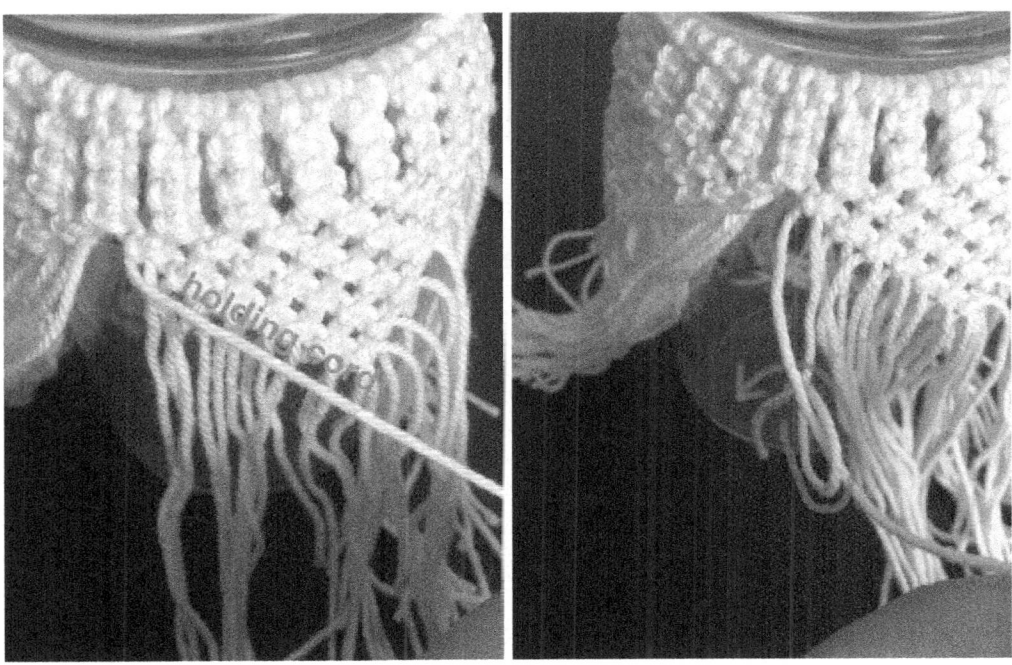

9. Take the extreme-left rope (holding rope) from the 1st left alternative square knot and positioned it above all other working cords diagonally. Take a functioning cord far left and create a counter-clockwise loop around the holding cord. Stretch securely on the functioning thread. Repeat to finish the dual half-hitch from the same cords. For all other operating cords, start double half hook. Thread 2 of the final alternating square knot (on top of the inverted triangle) is the only functioning thread.

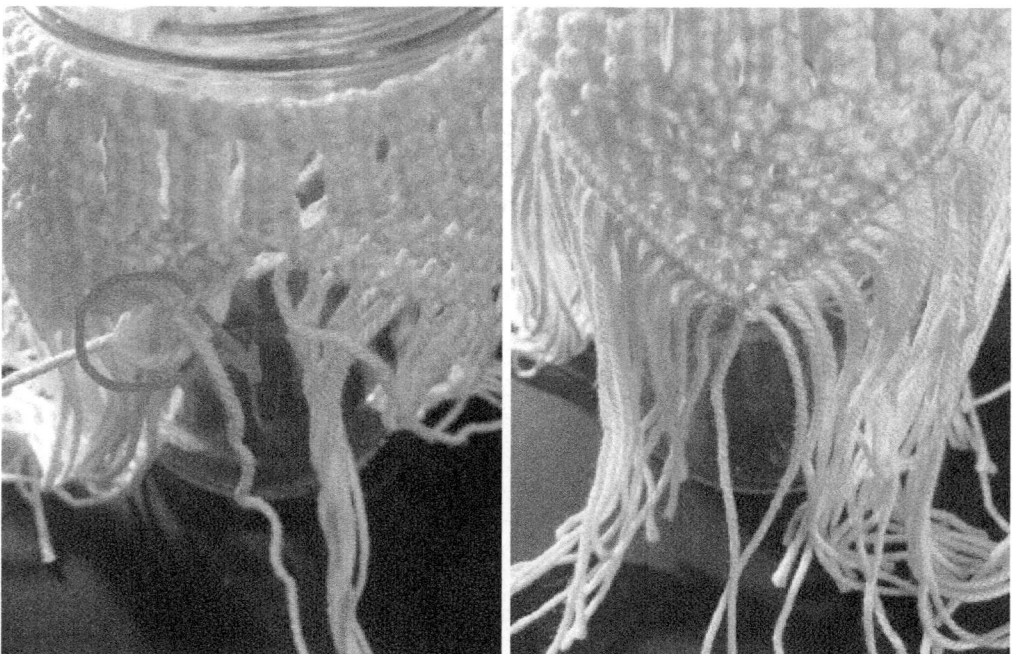

B) From right side to left side: Grab the extreme-right rope (holding rope) from the final right alternative square knot and position it above all other working cords diagonally (to the left). Take a functioning cord far-right and create a circle around the holding cord in a clockwise direction. Stretch securely on the functioning thread. Repeat to finish the dual half-hitch from the same cords. For all other operating cords, start double half hook.

Take the left cord and right cord to finish the arrangement, and render clockwise double half hook.

10. Cut both strings to ends.

Macramé fiber garland:

Things you're going to need:

• Thread

• Painters tape

• Scissors

• Image nails

• A clip to enjoy while you tie knots.

• Stage 1: Cut the important part of the yarn to the width you like. I cut these ones to 75 inches, by having in mind that 1 I would need around 5 inches for hanging on either end and 2) draping it will strip away most of its' breadth until I had installed the garland.

• Stage 2: Cut any single yarn pieces. I split my important part of yarn for 1.5 to see how much total yarn cuts I will like, as I needed about 1.5" apart for every product. I had in mind the colors that I needed to be highlights and the colors that I wanted to show more and split the cuts appropriately. I split every single piece to around 36" long to give plenty of space for failure, which was perfect because I made some mistakes.

• Step 3: Use tape for the painters to tape your main yarn piece. In your chosen order, add your fiber cuttings by making a single knot over the central part of the yarn. True talk: if you're saying, "Oh, this looks amazing already, and I don't feel saying making a lot of knots about few next hours," I'm not going to criticize. This is pretty good for me.

• Step 4: I couldn't do anything else, so I pushed forward. Tap the highest bit of yarn on the bottom left. Make a double knot in between the second and third yarn bits. I spaced my knots around 1 inch apart, but you might spread them further apart if you need a great transparent feel. Move on until you hit the correct leg.

• Step 5: Switch to the left side after you finish the first sequence, and begin again. Begin this time, on the far left with the initial piece of yarn. Again, bind double knots along this line before you get to the top.

• Step 6-Another band! Miss the first bit of yarn once again this time. Start by joining the third and second part of yarn with a double knot, then push all towards the right.

• Step 7: Cut the tails evenly, but don't be just like me. (Don't worry, the Windex took care of this.) As long as the yarn was still adorned, I trimmed them and resulted up with non-similar ends that I didn't understand until I put it back in my bedroom. I will recommend that you hang it straight over, and you can get a clear understanding of how both the tails are that's what I made at the end.

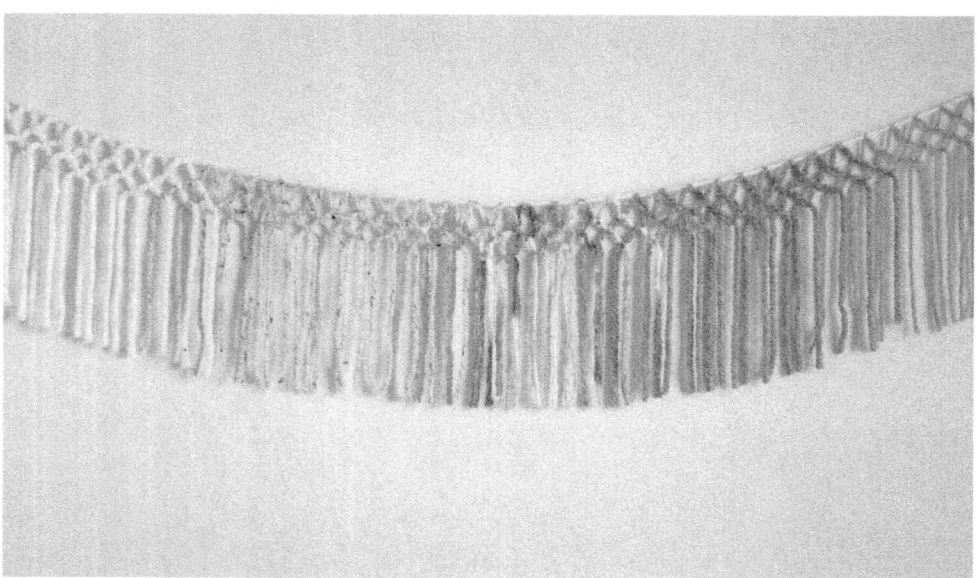

• Step 8: Put up the wall ish! I used a small nail at either end and then wrapped the thread across the nails.

Chapter 6: Wall hangings

The new trend in bohemian art has taken macramé along with it. Macramé is the practice of forming shapes by knotting rope or string, which was all the rage in the 1970s. Such elaborately designed items make a return and can be found everywhere. Check your hand at DIY macramé if you want to adopt this bohemian look at no expense.

At first, Macramé may sound like an intimidating technique, so we built a macramé wall dangling DIY, for example. The macramé tutorial uses only four specific forms of macramé knots, and we provide step-by-step guidance on how to build each. We have also added inspiration in design to show you how to view this special wall dangling macramé.

For beginners:

Knots you may require:
• Head Knot (Lark's)
• Squared Knot
• Double Half hitch knot
• Double Squared Knot

Lark's head knot making process method

First Step: Split the rope in half.

Second Step: Drive away from you and over the edge of the circle (ring or dowel), the folded side of the string.

Third Step: Thread through the loop to the ends of the chord and pull close.

Squared Knot Bind process:

First Step: Put four cords before you.

Second Step: Cross the two middle cords over the rightmost rope to create a "D" pattern.

Third Step: Pull the leftmost rope toward you and then guide it through the middle of the "D" shape below the end of the rightmost rope, behind the two middle cords.

Fourth Step: Cords tighten.

Fifth Step: Repeat, this time beginning with the rope to the left. Guide the right-most rope behind two cords in the middle and through the shape "D."

Sixth Step: Bind the knot.

Double Squared Knot Bind process

Each knot is similar to the squared knot but has only half as many Binds.

First Step: Set eight cords in front of you.

Second Step: Cross the two most rectangular cords over the four middle cords to form a "D" form.

Third Step: Gently draw the two leftmost cords towards you and then lead them under the end of the two rightmost cords, four cords behind the back of the middle, and into the point created by the two rightmost cords.

Fourth Step: Cords tighten.

Fifth Step: Repeat, beginning this time with the two cords to the west. Direct the two right-most cords behind four cords in the middle and through the "D" form in the center.

Sixth Step: Bind the knot.

A Double Half Hitch Knot

We will be wrapping this knot around a hoop and at a diagonal in this macramè tutorial.

First Step: Start by dangling your rope from behind the hoop.

Second Step: Take the rope end, draw it toward you, then hook it over the hoop and drag it to your left.

Third Step: Repeat this step again, pulling the rope's end up through the loop you created.

Fourth Step: Tighten the knot.

Macramé Wall Dangling Tutorial

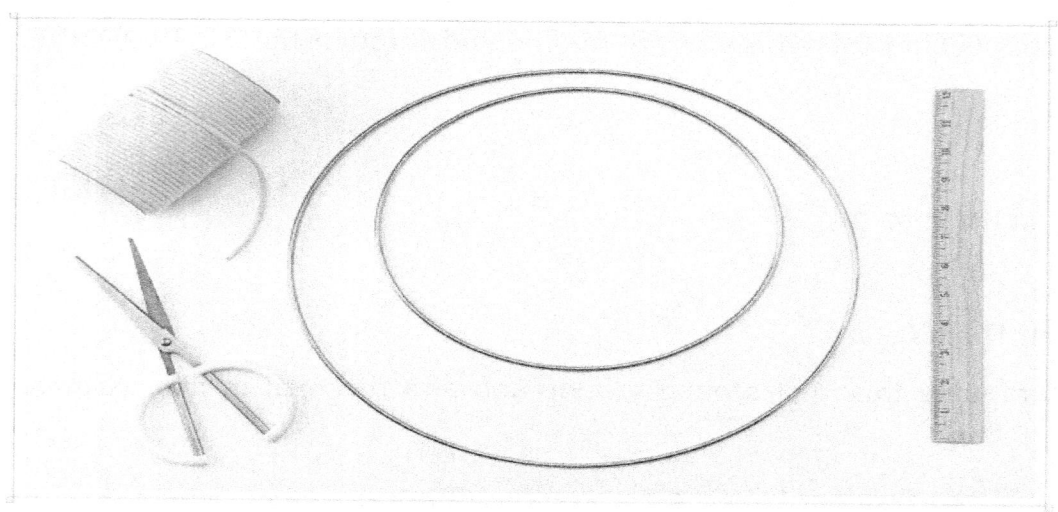

What you'll need:

• 160 foot (3 mm thick) of macramé string

• Scissors

• 10-inch gold hoop

• 14-inch gold hoop

• tape measure

First Step: Split the macramé rope into 16 10-foot parts.

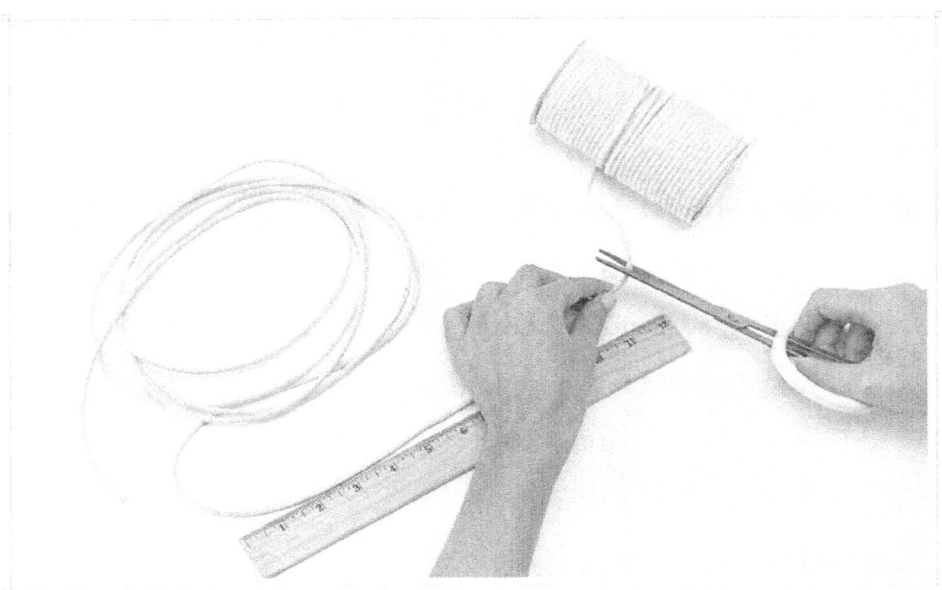

To weigh 10 feet of a chord using the tape measure. If you break one portion, you will use it to weigh the remainder.

Second Step: Add the head-knots of 16 larks to the 10-inch hoop.

Fold a rope section in two, then Bind the head knot of a lark around the 10-inch net. Repeat that for all 16 macramé rope parts.

Third Step: Generate seven rows of square knots and alternate between 7 and 8 knots.

When following this tutorial, the 1st rope is the leftmost rope.

First Row: Begin with 1st Row — Bind 8 square knots

Second Row: begin with 3rd Row — Bind 7 square knots

Third Row: continue with 1st Row — Bind 8 square knots

Fourth Row: continue with 3rd Row — Bind 7 square knots

Fifth Row: continue with 1st Row — Bind 8 square knots

Sixth Row: begin with 3rd Row — Bind 7 square knots

Seventh Row: begin with 1st Row — Bind 8 square knots

Eight Row: start with 8 square knots.

Fourth Step: Bind each of the 32 cords with a double half hitch knot to the bottom of the 14 "hoop.

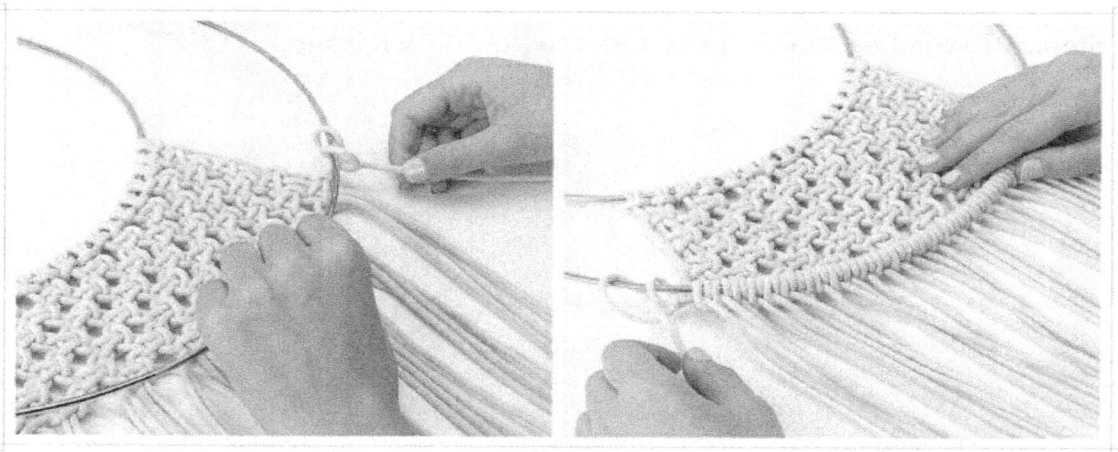

Ninth Row: Continue with 1st rope — attach 32 knots to the hoop with a double half hitch.

Fifth Step: Proceed for 16 more rows to Bind square knots and double square knots.

Ninth Row: Start with 1st rope — Bind 8 square knots

Tenth Row: begin with 3rd rope — Bind 3 square knots, skip four cords, Bind 3 square knots

Eleventh Row: begin with 1st rope — Bind 3 square knots, skip eight cords, Bind 3 square knots

Twelfth Row: continue with 3rd rope — bind 2 square knots, skip two cords, bind one double square knots, skip two cords, Bind 2 square knots

Thirteenth Row: start with 1st rope — Bind 3 square knots, skip 8

Sixth Step: Add 16 diagonal half-hitch knots beginning with the right-most thread.

A half-hitch diagonal knot is the same as a normal one, except instead of tying it around the hoop you are Bind it around another loop. Take the rightmost chord (32nd) and transfer it to the left over the other cords. Begin with the 31st string, and attach the 32nd string with 15 half hitch knots.

Twenty-fifth Row: Continue with the 31st string — attach 15 half-hitch knots diagonally to the center.

Seventh Step: Add 16 half-hitch knots diagonally beginning with the leftmost thread.

Repeat on the opposite side of the previous move. Cross the leftmost chord to the right over the strings, then add half knots to the string.

Twenty-sixth Row: Begin with 1st rope — Bind 16 half-hitch knots diagonally to the right.

Eights Step: Trim the end of the cords.

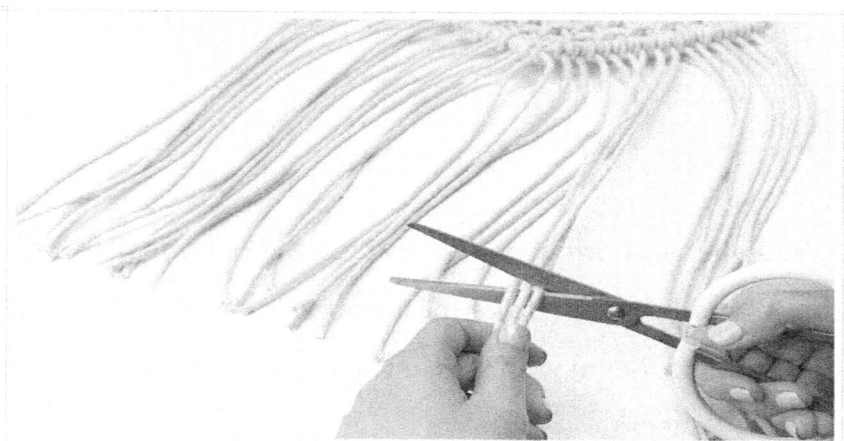

Ninth Step: Hang and enjoy!

For intermediate/advanced

1. Macramé Headband

We're beginning with a trendy headband to continue with our first intermediate project concept, macramé. I created this idea to wear to a music festival in early summer 2019. I've always adored the boho-chic feel and what better way to build my own sense of style than my own headband macramé

Inside the music festival scene, these macramé headbands have become quite popular, particularly among the hip and fashionable, boho-chic fashion crowd. I never ended up going to the music festival, but not all of it was lost, as I ended up wearing everything all summer long as it was the perfect accessory for any outfit.

This project may seem fairly easy to do to the naked eye, but the challenge of this project occurs when you need to create the design of heart jump. This is a case where only two knots are used, but the design itself is not straightforward. The more you learn various forms of using a knot, and the patterns it can make, the more you can improve your skillset for macramé.

This project is estimated to take around one hour to complete. The time will vary acropeing to the skill level and experience. To get going on this project, you need the supplies below.

Macramé materials required:
• Cotton rope 3 mm or 4 mm
• Elastic headband
• Thread and needle.

Length of Cords:
• 2 x 300 cm
• 1 x 150 cm

This is a perfect intermediate macramé project to get going if you're into boho-chic styling like I am. I would encourage you to take your time and go gradually while you're stitching the elastic headband to the template to prevent any problems or mishaps.

2. Macramé Necklace

The next concept I would like to share with you about the project is a macramé bracelet. This was another idea that I created, which I wanted to carry if I had the chance to join the music festival. I don't normally do things like this much, but I was on a boho design knotting binge during that specific month.

If you love DIY fashion shoes, handcrafted jewelry, or decorative art, you'll concentrate on utilizing a smaller rope length in diameter. The sort of rope I used for that particular project was a 1 mm cotton string. In my project, I have used sequins and beads and used 4 knots to create a distinctive style and look at the design.

For this project, I used sequins and beads; however, you may replace them with any other materials you can choose. You may attach buttons, charms, or any other items that will render it beautiful in its own right.

Don't be scared to go all out and do new stuff on several of those designs. You will discover quickly what you enjoy making and your own artistic style.

This project would require:

Macramé Supplies Required:

• 1 mm single strand rope

• Sequins

Cords length:

  • 6 x 240cm

3. Macramé Dreamcatcher

Dreamcatchers are a very different type of antique ornamentation. Originating from the Native American culture, they are considered to be holding supernatural forces. They are usually made of natural fibers bound together around a wooden hoop to create a pattern that is net or web-like. They're supposed to possess magical abilities that will fend off evil forces and preserve your dreams ... so that's exactly why I created one. Spirituality has always fascinated me, and it was natural that I fused a dreamcatcher with my passion for macramé. A few months ago, I created this dreamcatcher, and I want to share my experience on how I placed it all together so that you can build your own.

Dreamcatchers have now become a common piece in household decor, both indoors and out. Perhaps you can see them dangling in a nursery over a baby crib, or dangling above a wind chime outside.

They create some beautiful house decoration, and I think all macramé artists will strive to make one in their macramé journey, at least once.

Macramé Materials Required:

- 19 cm Metal loop
- 3 mm Cotton string (approx. 35 m)
- Metal comb
- Scissors

Rope length measurement:

- 1 x 300 cm (chain wrap)
- 8 x 350 cm for the remainder of the dream catcher.

The project will take around 1 -2 hours, so once it's done, you'll have a lovely dreamcatcher that you can put over your bed to help you sleep comfortably and shield yourself from any nightmares. Go ahead and give it a shot.

4. Macramé Flower

Aren't they pretty flowers? For them to attract your attention, they don't always have to be true.

Having flowers attached to my macramé designs is one of my favorites. It really puts the accent on what you made. You'll notice that incorporating different flower design types and leaf/feather designs would help your project come alive.

Personally, I like to add a variety of different macramé flowers to my wall dangling pieces, and I like to combine them with other natural macramé shaped patterns like feathers or leaves, too.

I wouldn't see this idea as being particularly complicated. I'd placed this project between the moderate and advanced levels of ability. The difficulty that I faced with this specific project was the number of knots I was expected to create using these thin strings to shape the flower design. While not a big concern, you would note that utilizing smaller diameter size rope on a project such as jewelry – bracelets, necklace and related macramé flowers like this one, you would need to take almost as much time, if not longer, creating such smaller projects relative to those of a medium or larger project utilizing thicker cords such as a macramé plant hanger or wall dangling.

Nevertheless, studying how to create a macramé flower can help significantly boost your endurance, binding strategies, and allow you the experience of building on your macramé base.

Macramé Materials Include:

• 1 mm cotton string

• Scissors

• Measuring tape

• Crochet Needle (optional) To get going on this macramé flower design, you'll need the following:

Range of Cords:

• 8 x 200 cm string of 1 mm cotton rope

• 1 x 1 mm hole (or larger) beads

Attempt to create a couple of these macramé flowers and get a better understanding of how this design is produced.

5. Macramé Book / Magazine Holder

Are you the kind of person who likes to get lost in a good book?

A decent novel in which you can't put it down and lose half the time? This macramé book holder project could be the ideal DIY macramé project for you if you love reading simply like I do.

I did this project because I wanted to introduce some type of exclusive house decor to my bathroom, I wanted to put up something that was beautifully pleasing and give the character of space and a little of my personal touch.

I began this project by pulling the head-knots of Lark over a wooden dowel. Instead, I started developing the book/magazine holder with the use of 2 knots, the Squared knot, and the Clove hitch knot to make a special template. The lower portion of the design was rolled up with the sides knotting together, making a wide enough pocket to accommodate a pair of magazines or books.

Expect to set aside roughly 2-3 hours from start to finish to render this possible.

Macramé Materials Need:

• 3 mm Single Cotton Thread String

• 12" Wooden Dowel / Rod

Cords length:

  • 24 x 300cm strands of rope

6. Macramé Garland

As we work through these concepts for a macramé project, you will begin to find that certain larger parts of macramé are more complicated and challenging to create. You'll need to find a convenient and wide enough area that either helps you to spread out the piece or operate on it or has a shelf that's big enough to carry the piece on.

If you are living in a tiny living room, making enough room may get difficult. I think what fits better for me is operating in an open area on a wide dining room table next to a basket with all my cords and materials. I always enjoy sitting next to a window to have the perfect sunshine and the comfort of the sun falling upon me. This makes for a fun and satisfying office.

It is a very long piece sitting over my fireplace now. Throughout this project, I used one knot in my project to create a bunch of leaf-shaped designs. The idea took me from start to finish in simply two hours. Yet after it's over, it's going to be completely worth it.

Macramé Materials Required:

• A 4 mm cotton string spool

string length:

• 1 x 155 cm

• 2 x 120 cm

• 4 x 60 cm

• 60 x 80 cm

• 10 x 100 cm

7. Macramé Tote Bag

If you 're trying to create a project that's functional and sustainable, a macramé net bag could be the perfect project for you.

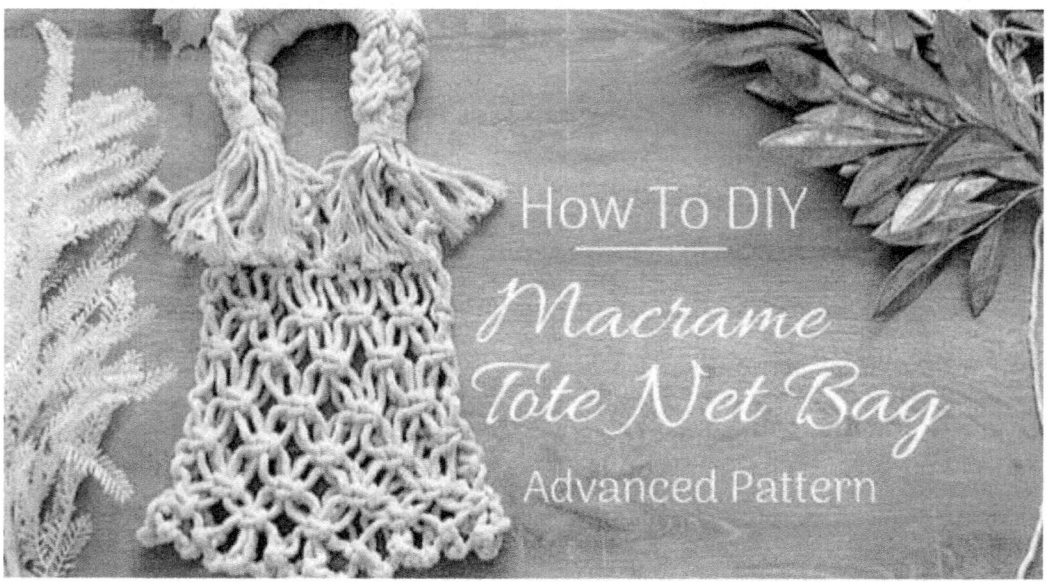

I created myself a macramé net bag early this year. I am striving to be more socially conscious of what I'm getting and what I'm using. I always tried to do my bit on the planet and get rid of as much plastic usage as I could, and what better place and continue with than shopping bags.

This was a project where, in tandem with my passion for macramé, I used some creativity to build something that would have an environmental effect. This is a wonderful idea that you should undertake if you choose to minimize the usage of disposable bags and move towards reusable bags as well. You might notice that the distance between the Binds might be a little wide for this specific project, so putting other things inside could cause it to fall out. You should attach a plastic cover to the side to prevent this so that the products don't spill out.

Another field of difficulty that certain people also face is the development of handles and their addition to the container. It can get a little complicated here, but you shouldn't have any trouble if you take your time and obey the video tutorial.

Give this project a try if you like the concept of combining art with a prominent cause!

Macramé Components Required:

Small size – 22 cm broad and 44 cm long (with handle)

- 4 mm Single Strand Cotton Rope Length:
- 20 x 250 cm
- 2 x 300 cm
- 4 x 40 cm Large size – 30 cm wide and 50 cm long
- 4 mm Single Strand Cotton Rope Length:
- 32 x 300 cm
- 2 x 350 cm
- 4 x 50 cm

8. Macramé Bedroom Wall Dangling

It's where I get the most pleasure when designing macramé to make bigger designs that require more knots to be able to come up with your own special template. You get a really satisfying feeling when you come up with an idea and go on with it all the way around. There is a deep feeling of contentment and happiness.

I decided to take a retro macramé piece for this macramé project and transform it into a new macramé house decor I could put up over my headboard in my bedroom. I've opted for a neutral beige cotton rope rather than utilizing traditional, rusty paint rope; (I think this beige neutral rope suits my style). I shaped the design to create this bedroom wall hanger by using 6 knots – the Lark's Head Knot, Berry Knot, Clove Hook Knot, Squared Knot, Josephine Knot, and the Gathering Knot.

You would require the following supplies to start this project: Macramé Supplies Needed:

• 4 mm Single Strand Cotton Rope

• Wooden Dowel 36″ inch

Long Cords:

• 15 x 300 cm

- 14 x 280 cm
- 12 x 250 cm

9. Macramé Lantern / Chandelier

We have now entered our final goal, a lantern of macramé. To anyone seeking to further zero in on their macramé skills and move your macramé abiliBinds to the next stage, I will highly advise you to pursue challenges that will get you out of your comfort zone to try something different.

The only path to get better is through continual learning and continuous development.

That's simply what I did when I challenged myself to design and create a macramé lantern that was completely original, and unlike every other project, I had created before.

It is an ambitious effort, which took me a few hours to finish. Well over 4 hours, so who's keeping track ... The fun part of this project is going around the ring of knots and making a 3D dimensional template. All of the macramé designs I've discussed above are 2-dimensional; anything can be achieved with the product lying flat. When you're working on a 3-dimensional layout, you'll continuously push the object around, swap places, and twist and transform while you create the design. It's safer to put the workpiece on a revolving double ended swivel ring rack for these kinds of tasks. This is going to make things even better for you.

If you're trying to build something or anything like that, another place you should be vigilant about is understanding what segment you're creating and not messing up the number of knots while producing designs. As I decided to do this project, I made a few errors, not wanting to count all the Binds for the design I was attempting to create. I was forced to take a few steps backward and unravel, tying my knots again.

You'll deal with 5 knots for this one-the Gathering Knot, Lark's Head Knot, Clove Hook Knot, Squared Knot, and the Berry Knot. The project is quite lengthy and will come up with some difficulty. I suggest that you go slow to make sure any knot you create is balanced and right as you go through each segment. Though this is an advanced project, don't be intimidated by how complicated it may look.

There is a second section of this project that you can add to this macramé lantern on a larger piece at the edge. If you are interested, please hang out on Patreon's Bochiknot.

For this macramé Lantern project, you will need the following materials and supplies.

• 4 mm Single Strand Cotton Rope

• 16 cm loop (wood or metal)

Rope length:

• 1 x 60 cm

• 8 x 100 cm

• 40 x 200 cm

Chapter 7: Plant hangers

There are lots of ways to create a plant hanger with macramé. Some instructions are much more difficult and time-consuming to execute, however. Those macramé plant hanger designs for beginners are a great place to start if you want to create something simple and convenient.

These DIY macramé plant hangers come in a number of sizes and types, and with little or no practice, each design is easy enough to complete. There are also several creative embellishments that render your macramé project appear customizer and more polished.

Know, it's good to first practice some simple macramé knots on some spare pieces of rope before you make a plant hanger. Understanding the Binds should make the directions on macramé even simpler to follow.

F0r beginners:

HOW TO Create A DIY MACRAMÉ HANGER FOR PLANTS
MACRAMÉ HANGER FOR PLANT REQUIREMENTS:

- Three mm Macramé Rope (Natural Cotton)
- Six in Metal Gold Ring or any size you want
- Tray with Pot
- Stretch 'N Gro Miracle-Gro
- Scissors

First Step: Plants Transfer to Different Bowl.

Start by placing your plant in its new container. My Jasper, fiddle leaf fig, which I felt was beyond the place of not returning even later with the fresh soil repotting, shows signs of the new existence. I keep on faith! I'm going to keep updating on how Jasper is doing.

You're able to launch your macramé project whenever the plant is content in its new box. I've completed a lot of macramé projects in the past, but I'm certainly not an expert; hence this small hanger is probably a project that anybody should handle. I simply used two styles of macramé knots to create it, and I very like it simply looks easy.

Second Step: CORDS Cutting.

By slicing eight large chunks of the cotton thread, you can continue your DIY macramé plant hanger. Now I have to slice my chucks to 10 feet each for my hanger. It turned out that this was simply the right duration. My planting machine is a little bigger, so if you're dealing with the smaller bowl, the parts might be smaller. Loop them around the gold hoop until you got the eight lengthy strands to be certain they turn it over hoop at the center point. Now you'll have sixteen long rope bits dangling from hoop down.

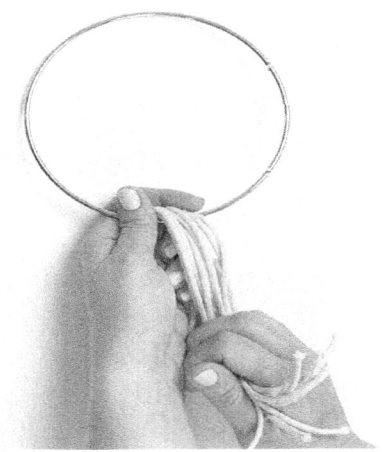

Third Step: KNOT Wrapping

Now, we can use a wrapped knot to lock these in a place. It's a basic knot with a finished, polished look. For that knot, you'll require another portion of the thread. I utilized one which was around 2 feet lengthy.

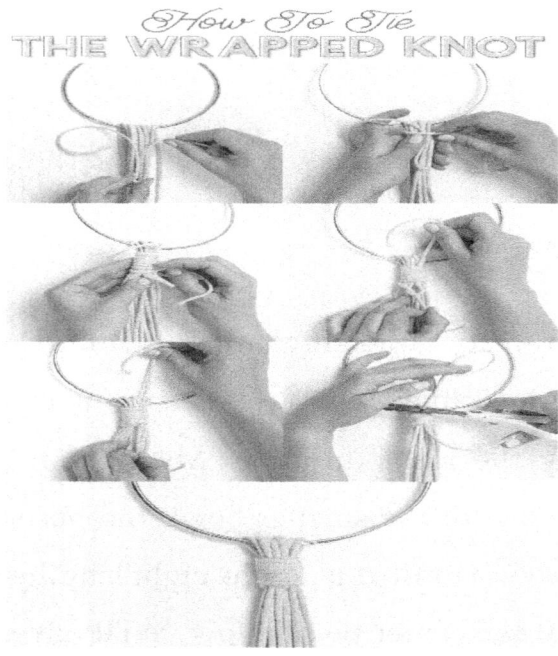

BINDING THE WRAPPED MACRAME KNOT

1. Put the small rope alongside the small tail to the left side of the spiraled cords, a spiral indicating downwards with the large tail to the right side.

2. Place the large tail over the cords looped, and the small rope loop.

3. Start winding the long neck, pulling closely, and uncovering the small rope loop at the edge.

4. Once you're pleased with the duration of the wrapped bind, run the large tail down the rope.

5. Bring the small tail up to close the bind and lower it inside the wraps.

6. Clip as similar as possible to these knots at the paws.

And it is! I adore how simple it is to make this knot and how great it appears when done. I think I'll use that for tassel creation in the coming days.

Fourth Step: ROW 1 OF SQUARE KNOTS.

We'll do a series of square knots next up. Begin by splitting your 16 strings into sets, everyone with strings.

Each one of 4 sets, we must function two square knots. I utilized a tape for measuring and calculated the equal distance from the bundled knot to each line of cords to keep them equally distributed across the planter, then outlined it with the pencil. I was about twenty inches for my first set of square knots for my hanger. Every set of four threads will be divided into the two outer cords used to bind the knots & these two middle cords that will bind the knots together.

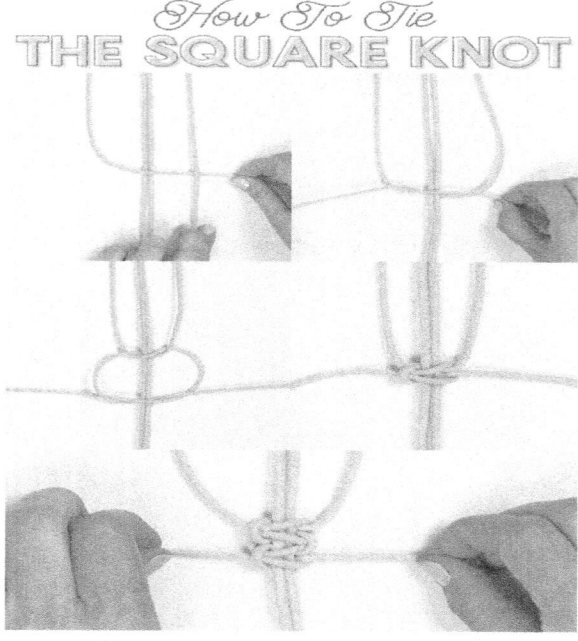

HOW TO BIND A MACRAMÉ SQUARE KNOT?

1. Place the left rope over the cords in the middle, and right under the string.

2. Loop the correct rope under the cords in the middle and above the wrong cable. Pull the knot to close, line it to the measurement point.

3. Undo this cycle moving in the reverse direction: Place the correct rope over the cords in the middle and to the correct under the cable. Loop the left rope below the cords in the middle and above over the right cable.

4. Zoom in to close. Shaped squared knot.

5. Repeat with two square knots to make.

Follow certain measures to establish two square knots at the same length from enfolded knots over each four-strand array.

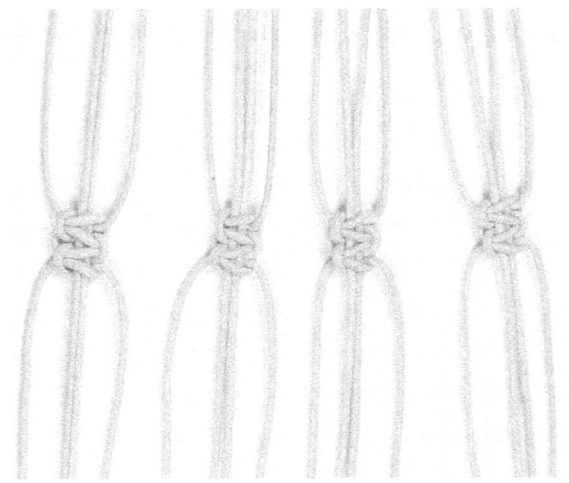

FIFTH Step: Square knots 2nd Row

We'll then render another series of square knots slightly beneath our 1st one. These knots are to be rendered over new four-strand pairs. From neighboring sets of 4, you must take two cords each – one main rope and one main rope on the right and one middle rope on the ground and the other on the bottom. Measure how much you like the next knots to fall beneath the last row of knots. I thought my planter should look fine around 5 inches down.

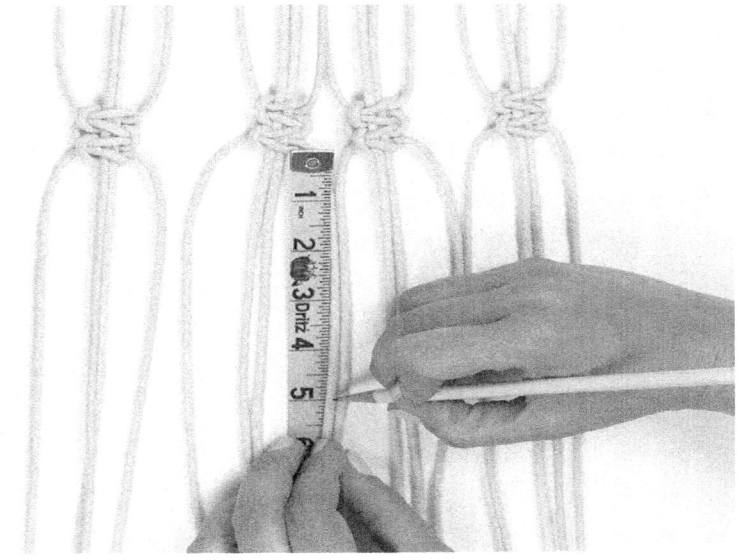

Next, Bind two square knots over those new four-strand groups at the measured mark.

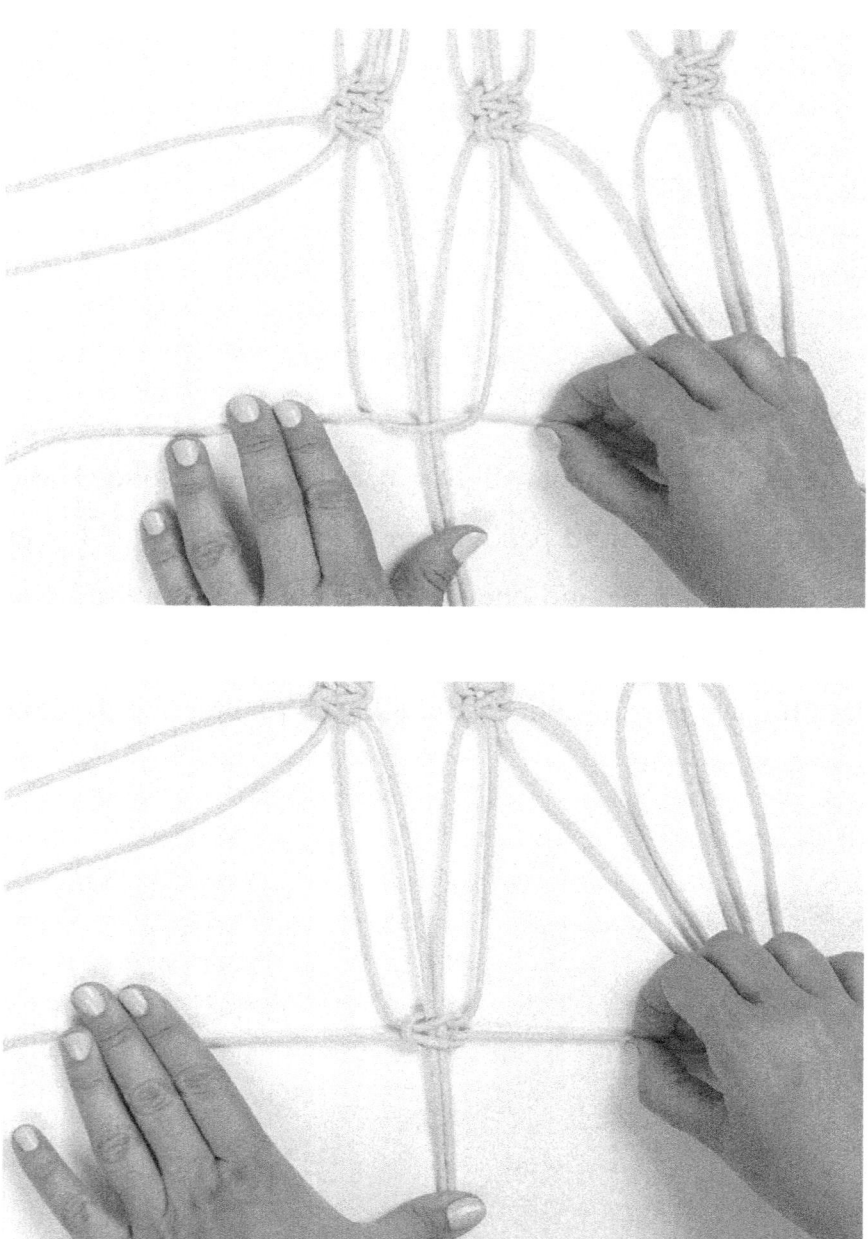

Your effort would be creating a sort of tube at this stage, so you'll have to spin the effort over to join the final four-strand section.

SIXTH STEP: FINISH KNOT AND CUT

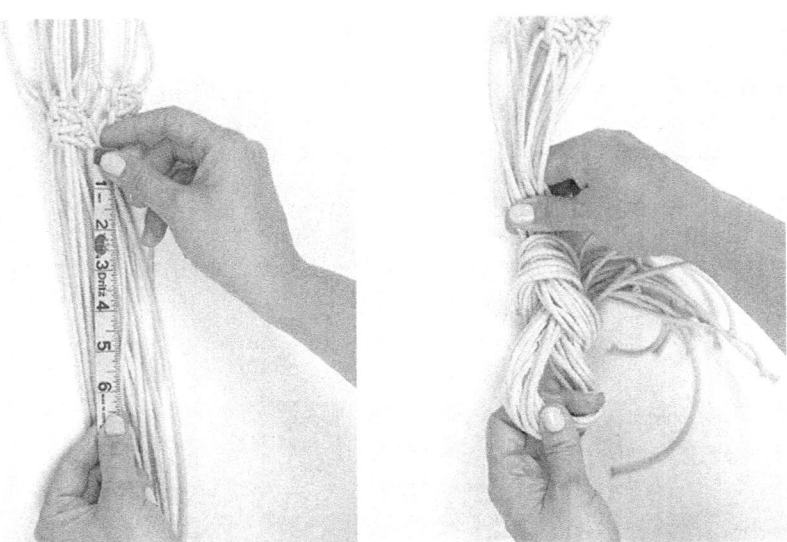

You'll be required to bind all the cords along with one last knot to finish off your DIY macramé plant hanger. Measure how much below the 2nd knots row you like to make the final knot. I put mine simply under 7 inches. To Bind and lock the knot, thread all the cords closely and rally them out—trim cords to make the ends straight out.

SEVENTH STEP: HANGING OF THE PLANTER

Now, things which remain to do is mount and put up the planter. Carefully arrange the divisions of your plants between the chord classes and ensure that hook on which you are going to mount the planter is firmly fixed to the roof and ready to support the weight of the plant.

Advanced/intermediate:

This Summer Macramé was in vogue; however, they may be pricey for the bind plant hangers; moreover, as I'm truthful, at first sight, they seem to be difficult to DIY, although, with some training, they aren't difficult to create.

Don't let them trick you with Binds! I've always said one reason I'd never survive as my future relied on it; I may not get the knot from something. It's humiliating, and because of that, I realize I've missed great mom details, so knots seem to be my foe. Yet this time, it is not. I am going all in dry; there's going to be. Then let's carry on our macramé!

Materials:

• Three desired plants, I prefer succulents because they are less messy

• Clothes line / String

• Soil for Potting

• Three pots (smaller the better)

• chain- to put your final work in the sunlit place

• spade (gloves-optional) in case you require good fingernails.

First Step: Cutting

• Start by cutting off six threads of the equal length of rope. The duration of your plant will rely on how much low you require it to stay. For our hanger, we were doing 2½ arm spans.

• When you've had your six threads, bind them all together and make one huge knot This would be your plant hanger at the base.

Second Step: Knotting

- Once 1st knot is connected, divide the three cords in the set of two. It is what keeps the first pot at heart. Measure the pot's bottom by putting its core on its first, first knot.
- Then bind 3 knots over the outer side of the pot, which keeps and stabilizes the pot.

Third Step: Fitting

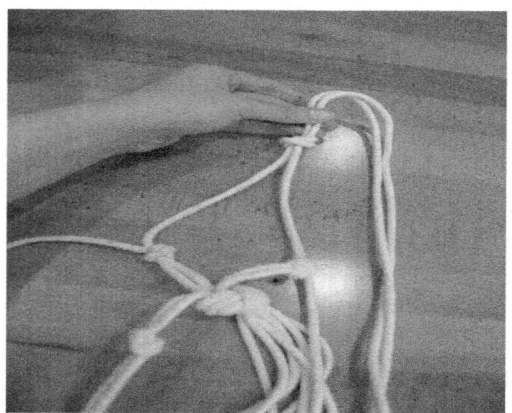

- After the first knot is formed, split the three strands into the sets of 2. That is what holds the first pot at the core. Measure the pot's bottom by placing the heart on the first, first knot.

- Then bind 3 knots across the outer edge of the pot and holds and stabilizes the pot.

(At this stage in training, here is how the rope will look like.)

Fourth Step: Knotting and Repeat

• After snugly putting your 1st pot into the 1st three bouts of binds, immediately detach the pot and perform the measures again.

· Later, you have calculated and bind all the knots, now create a single spiral knot at the edge so that you may hang the planter.

Fifth Step: Planting of Little Plants

• At this time for some fun! Transplant the tiny wee baby plants in the safe new houses.

* Be sure to utilize the soil made especially for succulents and cacti, if using succulents. It's not hard to locate any rocks for good drainage at the garden mostly and dump them into the base and across the corner.

• Other fun choices would be an ivy bush that drapes when it rises, or you might put some colorful pops in these to show the season. Clear orange or purple mums, zinnia coral, or white petunia fuchsia!

Sixth Step: Assembling

• Once all plants have been planted, the cycle of the assembly will begin. The aspect is very complicated. If you have the hook in-ceiling or the wall already ready, that should make the attachment even simpler.

• Hang up the string by a hook, now drop growing pot softly into its tiny rope nook.

Macramè

Chapter 8: Modern and fashion house macramé

Macramé, which is a flexible type of fiber art, can be used to create anything from wall dangling and plant hangers to shoes, purses, and even clothes. Although macramé became popular in the 70s with an incredible revival in recent years as interior decoration, knots have consciously made their way into fashion. Subtle is an underestimate as house-made knots surface on runways and on the worldwide farmers' markets. Visually stunning and expressive, in motion, macramé can become an entire show in itself. Thought about it by having portable macramé as another way to carry the job out into the community from your studio. Who wants a Visa Card? Create a statement necklace or a sassy top, and we're sure you'll love your job!

Adorable macramé top:

This project of not sew style is basic and gratifying. There is no need for special expertise or experience to render the cute peak. In the afternoon and happily wear it to a bar, swimming party, outdoor store, festival, show, etc.

First Step: Materials Required

Broad, t-shirt (tailored) (It will reach a couple of inches around your knees. I utilized a 100 percent cotton top. However, a cotton + nylon mix would function all right, too. Be certain to wash and dry the shirt if it's not pre-shrunk.)

Ruler

Pencil cloth scissors (a dark pencil if the top is white; a white pencil in case the shirt is black.

Second Step: Cutting of Sleeves and Hem off Shirt

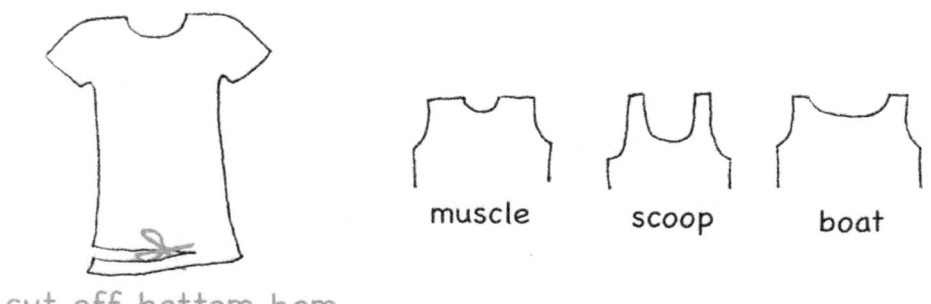

Cut the shirt's bottom fringe slightly behind the cuff stitching using cotton scissors. Then determine which design you want to see at the top of the tank. You should either use your pencil to spread the tank-top onto the shirt and sketch the outline, or you may devise the form (with the aid of a ruler to hold it even). I considered it useful to switch shirt inner side turned outward while improvising, because I might check the seams on the back. To obtain the top shape of the tank you like, cut the sleeves (and neckline if desired). I sketched some thoughts for top shapes for the tanks in the photo.

Third Step: Fringe Lines and Upper Limit Mark Fringe

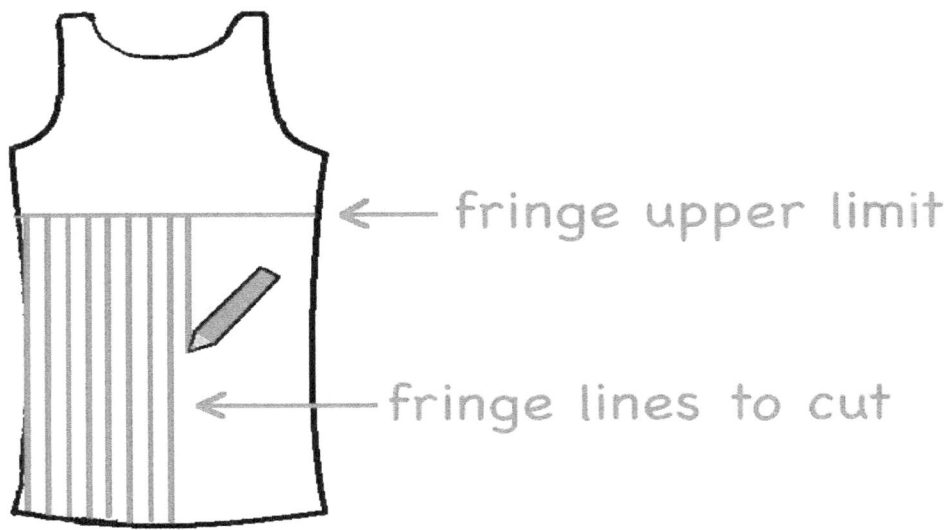

Wear the shirt and determine how big the fringe lines you need to run. I propose that the fringe be stopped a few centimeters under the bust. Using the pencil to spot where you will want. Taking off the jacket and put it upside-down with the chest face up. Make a straight line over shirt on the spot that you've outlined it with your ruler.

Decide now how broad you like your fringe stripes to be trimmed. Now cut half inch-wide stripes for my project and wound up having 32 strips around. To use the macramé method, I use in this tutorial, you need the overall amount of fringe stripes to be the multiplex of four. However, if you want to achieve the correct sum of stripes, you will need to change the bar wideness to 5/8" or 3/8". Well, I would not suggest deviating much from half inch-wide stripes. Using your pencil and ruler to map out the fringe lines, you'll break. Make sure you test for reasonable spacing the lines from bottom to top; this is easy to screw up.

Fourth Step: Fringe Cutting

Utilizing your rotary cutter or scissors to remove the fringe. When you cut all of the shirt's front and back right away, beware not to make the shirt's back slip out of a spot when you cut. In case the shirt has them, a notice regarding side seams: Well, I finish up removing the side (seams) because the rough stitching wouldn't fit as good as a fringe. If you do want to do so, make sure the cumulative amount of fringe stripes is also the multiple of four.

Fifth Step: Beading plan

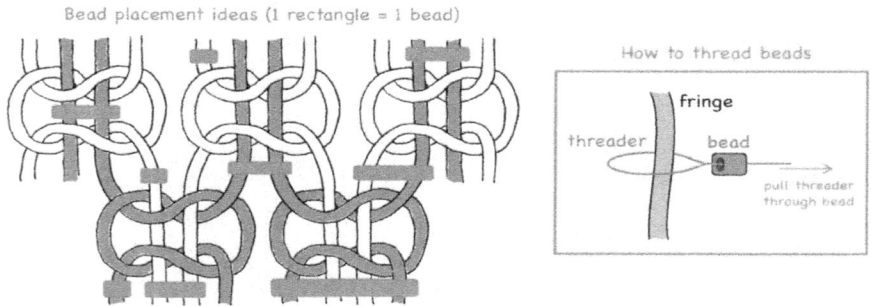

For suggestions about where to include beads in the macramé style, see the diagram. (This illustration will make better logic in the coming stage as the knot design is described.) You'll more definitely require the support of a threader if you slide more than two fringe stripes into one bead. There is an image in the figure which demonstrates how to do a bead threading. A notice on bead diameter, you require a bead hole size (diameter) of 6 mm (simply below 3/16) "to put two half-inch broad fringe stripes from it. In case you choose to put four half-inch broad fringe stripes from a needle, you need a needle hole of 11 mm (approximately 5/16 inches) in size (diameter).

Sixth Step: Binding of Macramé Knots

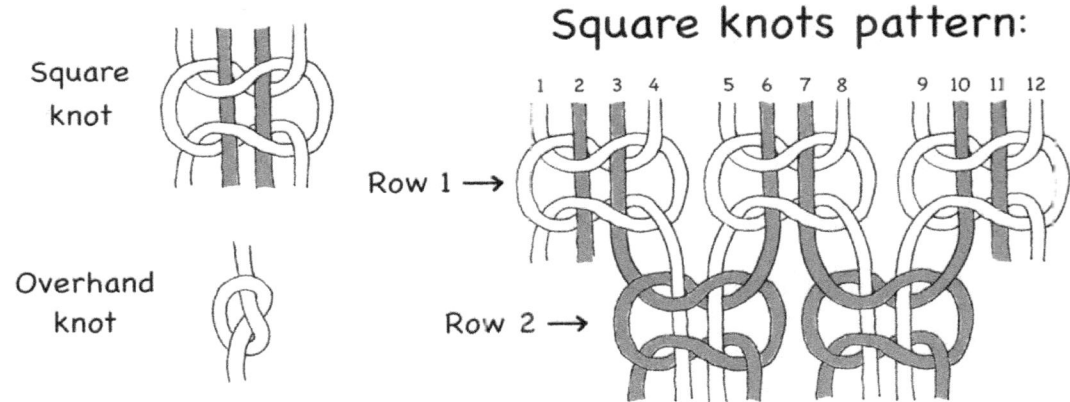

With the shirt spread front facing up and right side out, begin making square knots starting with far-left (or far-right) fringe stripe, which you removed from the front side of the top. Watch the figure for having one series of square knots all over the tank. Now, replicate for a 2nd row in a different design, as seen in the figure. (The fringe threads are represented in two distinct shades to minimize uncertainty over which threads are utilized where.) If applying beads to fringe beneath the squared binds, make sure to attach overhand Binds directly beneath the beads to prevent them from falling off the stripes (fringe). Note: Do not make the binds really strong whenever you are going bind them as you might want to make some adjustment while you move along to hold the job straight. When you're done with the Binds, go on and secure them.

Seventh Step: Instructions for care

I have no idea how far the knots in a laundry machine and dryer will go, so I suggest laundry the tank top by hand and putting it on a flat surface to dry.

Fashion purse from macramé

Components & Materials Required to create Macramé Purse.

- Plaited macramé rope 110 yards of 6 mm or 5 mm

- One-inched beads 20 (wooden) (Ten beads in the back, Ten beads in the front)

- Board for knotting or ceiling tile

- Scissors and T Pins

- Ruler, yardstick or tape measure

- design adhesive

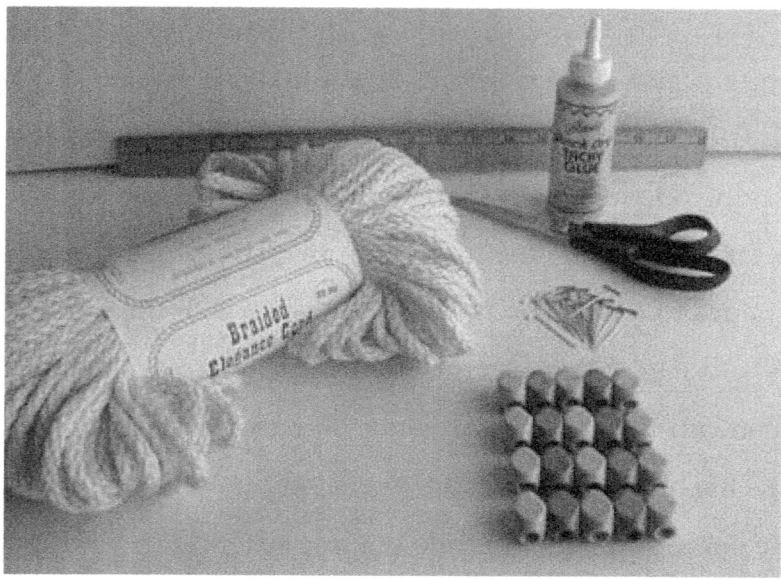

First Step: Slice the following cords.

- Thirty-Six cords 2 yards 6 inches long for body of purse

- Four cords 3 yards long for straps of purse

- Four cords 5 yards long for straps of purse

Second Step: Straps Making

Second, you are going to make 2 belts. Pin on knotting board the middle of 2 of the three-yard cords next to each other. Pin 2 of the five-yard cords centers at each hand of the three-yard cords. In this sequence, cords would be alienated. Rope 5 yd, chord 3 yd, chord 3 yd and rope 5 yd. The three-yard cords are filler strings, while the connecting strings are the five-yard cords. Place on the floor knotting with four ends rising up above the surface and other four falling down the wall. See diagram below.

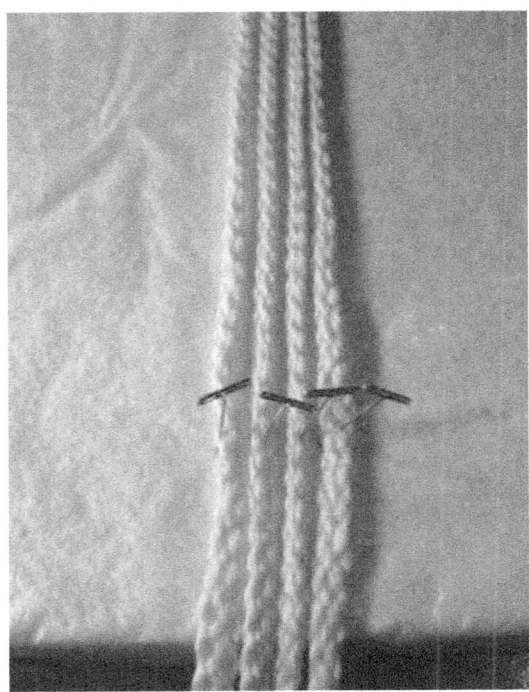

Function with those four strings binds a 10 Square knots (SK). Sinnet is the string with the same binds connected with the same connecting cords consecutively. For example. Turn the board to bind.

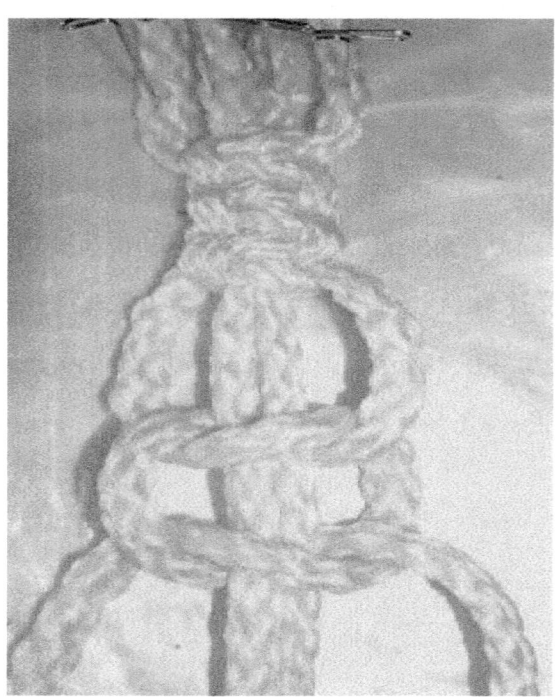

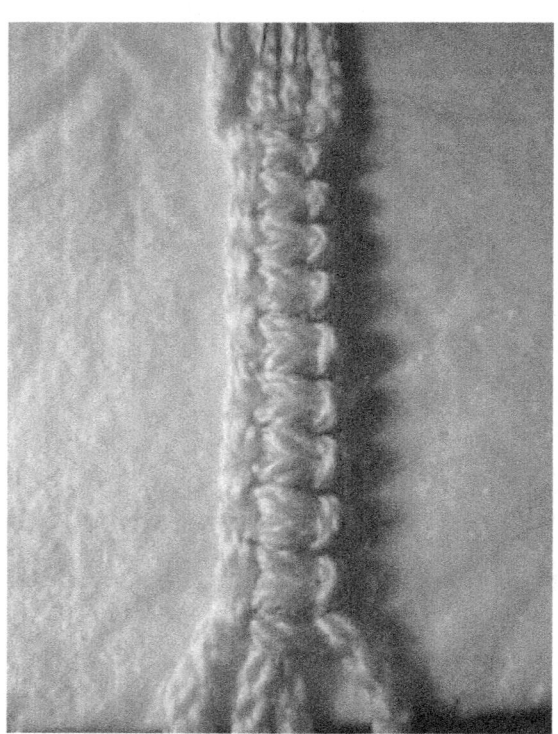

Keep connecting the Sinnet of fifteen HK (Half Knots) to the SK sinnet. After around the third HK. Half Knots should start twisting. That's fine; this will be finished.

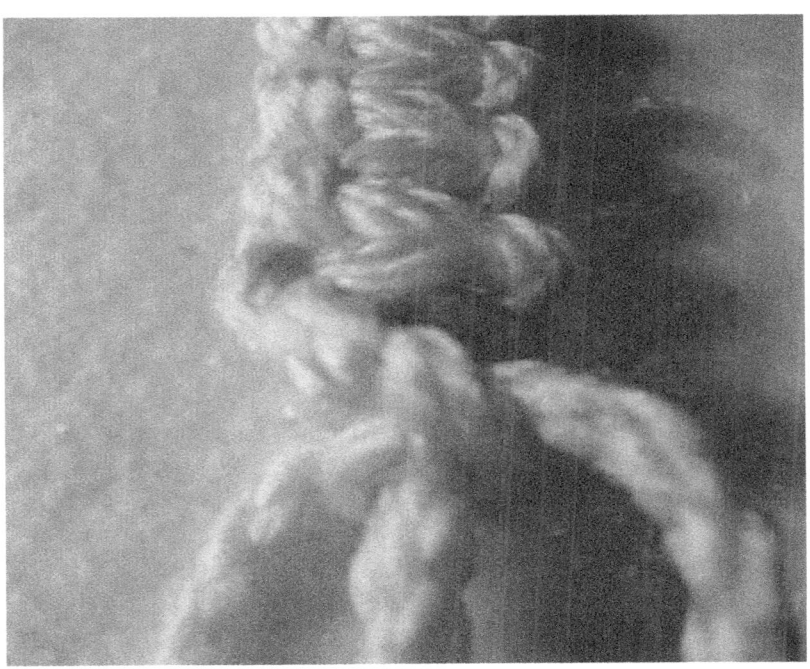

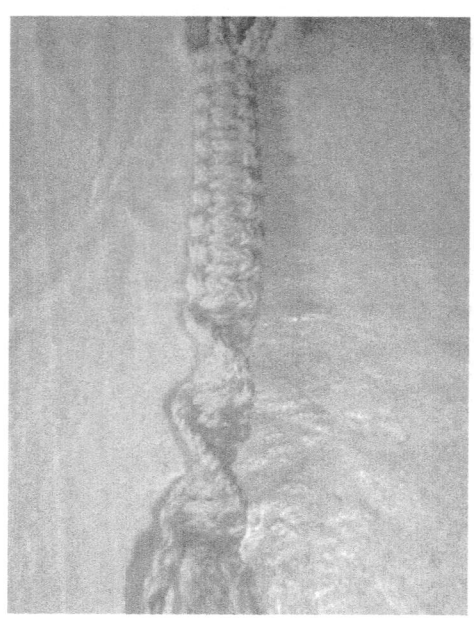

Turn strap and operate in another direction, proceed where you "finished." (Note: Bind an HK earlier than binding an SK. This finishes the knot binding first.) Now you're able to continue binding knots in that direction.

Undo rendering the same SK sinnet 10 knots and HK sinnet 15 knots as you were doing with the top halved of those four strings. This fills out the 1st brace. Now repeat 2nd strap operation. That is how they will feel at the two assembled Binds. Set aside braces.

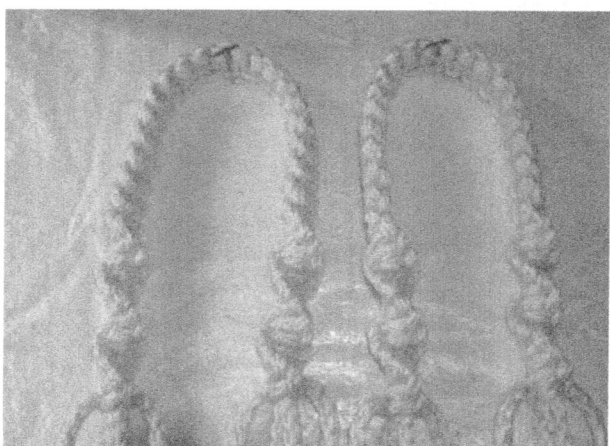

Third Step: Creating A Purse Front Portion

Fold 2 cords in half utilizing the two-yard 6 inches cords and pin the cores next to each other on the knotting surface. Fasten a Squared Knot (SK) with the four strings, taking the knot fully up to the T-pin and no loops would be over knots. Deposit back. Run the cycle again 17 times. You should have 18 Parts of the Squared Knot. (These eighteen would be indicated as 'Simple Knot Pieces' in this tutorial.)

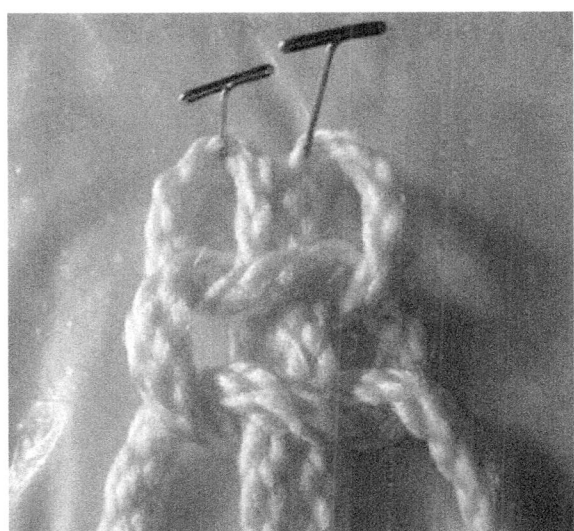

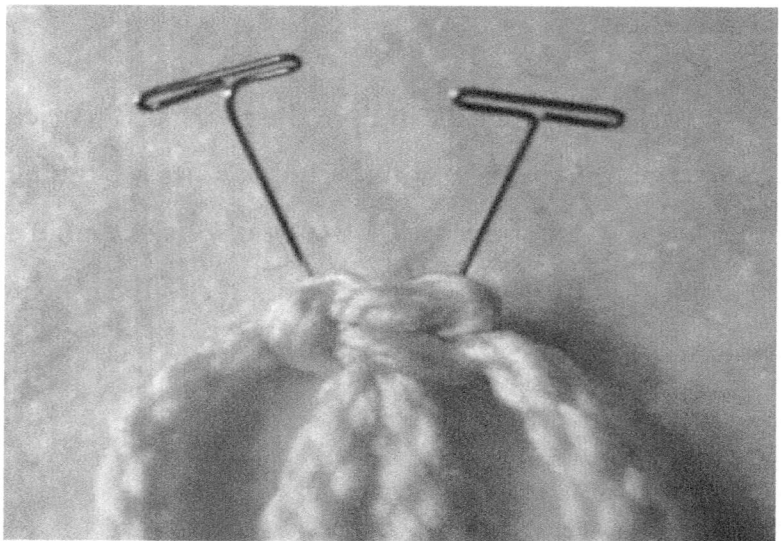

Now the sixth pin of the Squared Knot Parts generated next to each other in the last phase into the knotting wall. Bind them along with Alternating Square knots (ASK), beginning on the left with the third string. You are going to match 5 SK's in that section. Set the frame knotting on.

Fourth Step: Attaching the Strap to Purse Front.

Take one brace and bend it backward in a bow. Place one end of the head part of the purse (that is on knotting board) to the left and the different edge of the strap to the head part of the purse to the right. Connect one Squared Knot on the left with cords three to six, and nineteen to twenty-two on center. Drop rooted knotting. (Counting of cords may shift when parts are inserted, so only renumber mentally as counting is suggested in the directions.)

Fifth Step: Formation of Side

Attach three Squared Knot parts on board and bind them with a 2 ASK chain.

Do the same with three more Parts of the Squared Knot. Place 1 out of these parts on the left side of the purse strap after the knotting is done THAT IS ON THE KNOTTING BOARD and add the other part on the side. (Photo illustrates exactly how to connect this freshly formed portion to the right hand of the rope. Do the same for the left side.) Fasten both parts together with one Squared Knot, use two free cords from Square Knot Segment, and two from the brace. Take the screen off, then put back. Attach three Squared Knot parts on board and bind them with a 2 ASK chain.

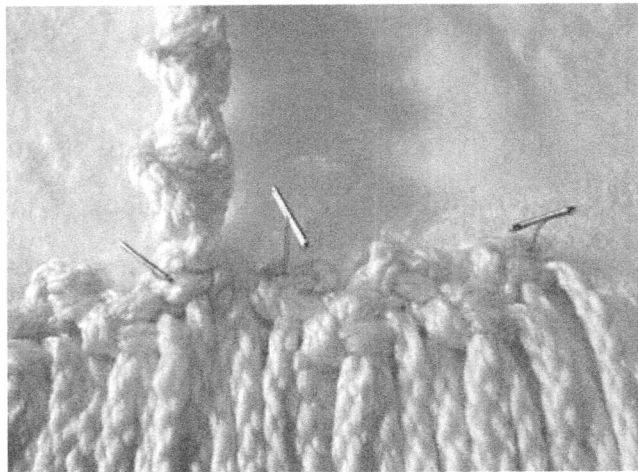

Yeah, let's do a recap of what you've accomplished up till now. The two loops are made, and the front portion and the two side parts have been fitted with one band. This is how you will look at this point from your bag..

Sixth Step: Second Strap Connecting & Creating the Back

Place 6 SK Pieces to Bind board next to each other, simply like you did with the end ... Bind them together with one series of ASK, beginning with the third rope on the bottom. You are going to match five SK's in that section. Set the frame knotting on. If you need support, refer to the knotting diagrams in Stage 3.

Take the 2nd brace and bend it backward in an arc. Pin one end to the left side of the purse back portion (which is on the knotting board) and the other end of the brace to the right-hand side of the purse back section. Note: Make sure that this brace weighs precisely the same as the first band. "Pull" back into the sinnet if appropriate to even bring it out.

Connect one Squared Knot on the left with cords 3 to 6 and 19 to 22 in the center. Drop rooted knotting.

Seventh Step: Sides to Back Joining

Connect the back with one SK to the side portions utilizing the two side free cords and two back part cords.

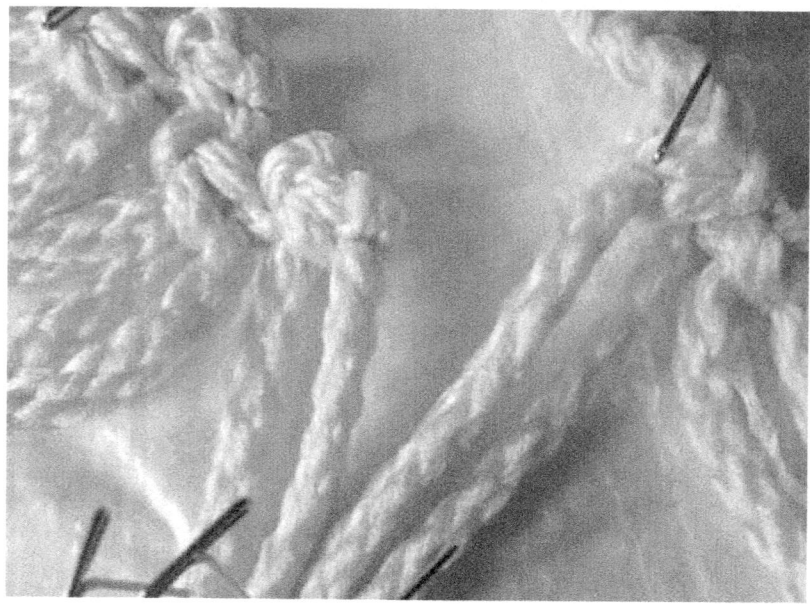

Repeat the process on the 2nd side as well.

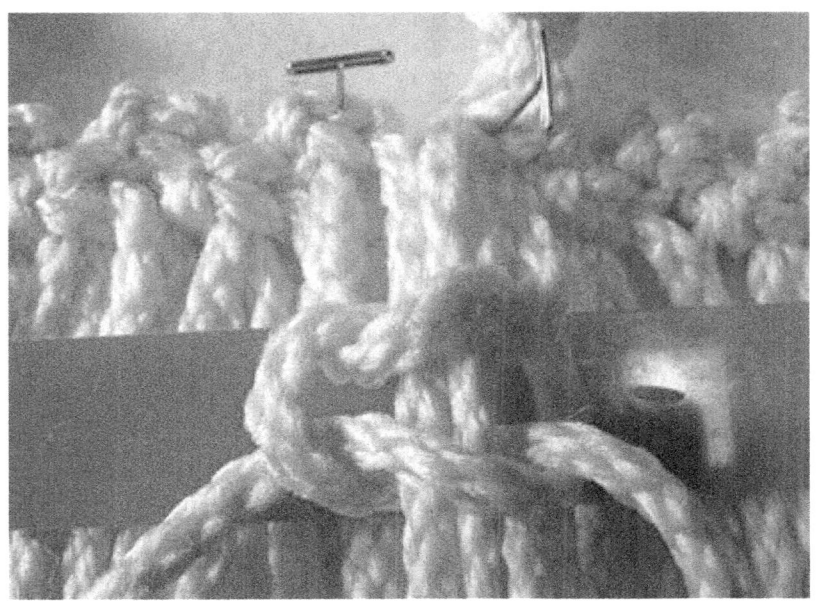

Now, you got a complete one row of Squared Binds running right over the entire bag.

Eight Step:

- You are going to be making knots rows of in a circle, tube format. Bind six rows of ASK (Alternating Square knots) in the order of:
- Third Row - Bind the row of SK
- Fourth Row - Bind the row of ASK
- Fifth Row- Bind the row of SK
- Sixth Row- Bind the row of ASK
- Seventh Row-Bind the row of SK
- Eighth Row- Bind the row of ASK

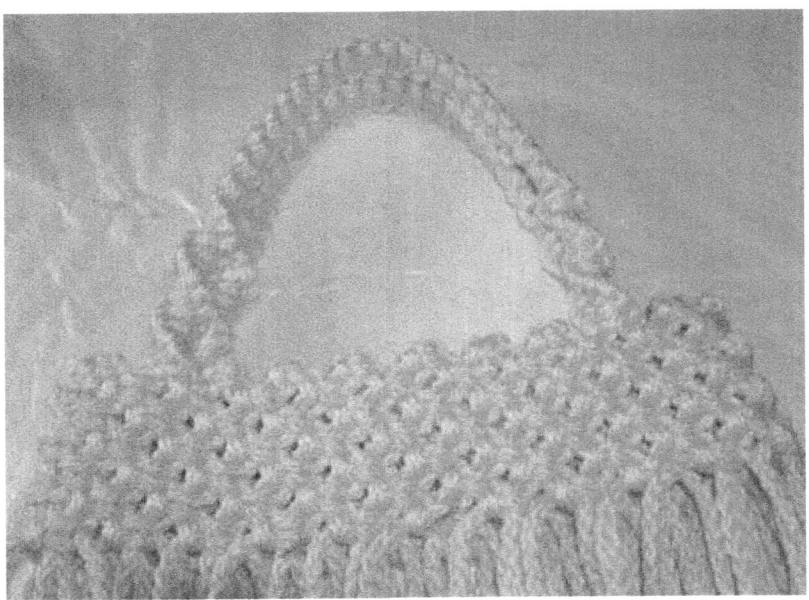

Ninth Step: Add Row 1 Beads Lines.

Now you are going to continue applying beads to the bag front. Number the cords 1-44 starting with the side knot halved. Attach a Squared Knot (SK) in five to eight, thirteen to sixteen, twenty-one to twenty-four, twenty-nine to thirty-two, thirty-seven to forty strings. The middle cables of the four strings placed a bead beneath every one of these SK's on two filler cables. Beneath every bead bind another SK, utilizing the equal four cords because for these knots over the beads.

Bind an eight halved Knots sinnet with the 9 to 12, 17 to 20, 25 to 28, and 33 to 36 strings. Repeat these actions by attaching beads to the purse back and binding half knot sinnets to it.

Tenth Step: Sides filling with Knots.

To fill up the opposite purse sides wherever beads are attached, attach four rows of ASK binds. The first row has one knot, the second row has 2 knots, the third row has 1 knot, and the fourth row has 2 knots. Set up these binds with this bead-sheet. (Note: Don't get on for the last two knots.)

Eleventh Step: Between the Two beads row, there is one set of Binds. Attach one Question group all over the bag.

Twelfth Step: Make the SECOND ROW. Repeat steps 9 and 10 to connect the beads in the second row and fill the side knots in. Back and front.

Thirteenth Step: Now, bind up five ASK rows all over the whole container.

Fourteenth Step: Base Closure.

First, switch incorrect purse side out to close the base of the bag. Move through the final knots row to ensure that the ties are very strong.

Place the purse sides straight on the floor. On each hand, you can see ONE SQUARED KNOT dividing the rear and front of the bag. Now, this is the place where you get to bind the bottom in—yeah, prepared? Place purse with bottom-up between your thighs.

Begin at the farthest (on the ground) 6 strings, attach 2 Squared Binds, use four filler strings and one rope from the bag left side, and one rope from the bag right side.

Continue to close the base of the purse by utilizing next two cords from the purse's Either Hand, then attach ONE Squared Knot really firmly.

Move to go through the base of the bag until you hit the other leg. It will have six cords remaining. Bind 2 Squared Binds for these six cords use four filler cords, and one rope from the purse left side and one rope from the purse right side as you do the same at the other hand of the bag with the six strings.

Fifteenth Step: Bottom Cords Cutting

This completes binding the knot. Apply glue to design on each knot. Leave to air. Cut the cords below, leaving around 1/2" behind. Melt the broken cords with a lighter cigarette to avoid fraying of cords. Keep blaze to the ends of the rope for simply a single second, and you won't damage the cords. Now you're able to transform right-hand side out bag. Prepare and attach the covering, if you so desire.

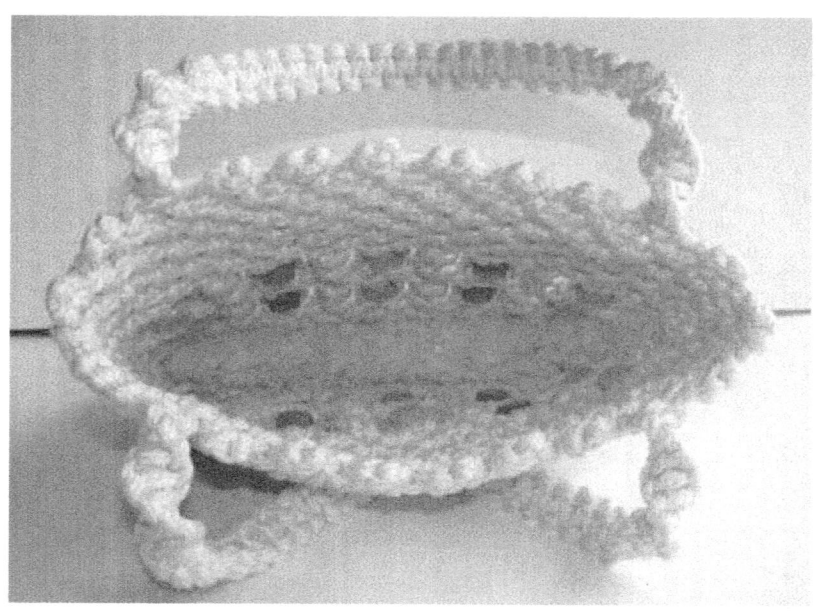

Chapter 9: Macramé garden project ideas

I enjoy dangling plants at my porch at the time of summer and spring months. It also gives it a very pretty look, and it's a perfect way to hold an eye on my more responsive plants. I have a nice little surprise for you if you enjoy dangling plants; however, I really don't want to waste the money on the plant hanger bought in store. I find twenty DIY dangling plantings, which are all very cheap and simple to create. You may hang them in the interior of your house or put these to the deck to put elegance and color to any space.

Plant hangers aren't hard to produce at all, and the stuff you can repurpose and revamp to create them really don't believe you. You can find the ideal dangling plant from antique cages of birds to empty coconuts to give the house the desired look you like. Dangling plants in the house not only put the appeal, but keeping those rising plants inside is very safe for everyone in the house. And, all of these are so simple that you may prefer to make all of them. They are guaranteed to make you improve your house lawn.

You don't even have to pay a lot or run yourself in desperation to have a wonderful garden and house. With simply a few bucks and some hours, you can make the very beautiful DIY dangling planters that will present such color and style to the porch and house! If you simply want to make your garden and house better this summer and spring, you simply need to try out some dangling planters.

1. **Easy Dangling Planter**
2.

In case you require something that is super simple and cheap, it's this dangling planter. You can do it with a cheap Walmart, Dollar, or Target Store planter and then only attach your dangling rope to it. Putting this one together takes only a couple minutes, and in case you decided to modify it a little more, you might paint whatever color you choose to suit your current decor to the planters.

3. **The planter of Revamped Bird Cage**

These cool antique cages can be sold in thrift shops, and these are very cheap. Do not worry if these cages have dents, even if they are little damaged even missing, that only put the charm of the rustic. Simply furnish it with the desired plants until you've got the cage and cover it with twine, rope or string. It is a smart place to get a gorgeous planter suitable for dangling indoors or outdoors.

4. Planter of Revamped Coconut

As I prefer fresh coconut; however, I don't know how to use shells except maybe chuck them away. That is a very safer concept here. Transform the shell of hollow coconut into a grower! You should simply create a coconut in two planters. These are great for succulents planting, or you may put a tiny floral house to them. When you're searching for a nice presence on the shore, coconuts may be the best dangling planters.

5. Planter of Dangling Beaded

Only the ten-dollar cost of supplies offers you everything you require to build a lovely dangling planter. To build this one, you need only a jar, twine or rope, and some fancy beads. It's super simple and simply takes a little amount of time to complete. These create great presents in case you know someone who enjoys dangling plants and adding some lovely greenery, they maybe hang them on the porch, indoors, or roof.

6. Upgrading of DIY Dangling Planter

With only a few materials and a little amount of time, take every ordinary dangling planter and transform it into something amazing. This is very gorgeous and simple to do. To make it beautiful you want a simple vine, and then a little paint with other decoration. You may do any style or paint scheme you require to suit your other decor.

7. DIY Dangling Wall Planters of Wooden

Well, you don't have to actually have twine or string to admire the lovely dangling planters. These walls of wooden planting devices are very simple to create and cheap, and also, they stick straight on the walls. Moreover, these are perfect for succulents planting, or you might give them a bigger one and bring in the larger plants. Hang them in the building, or on a porch or roof. To spread out your yard, hang it closer to the succulent DIY garden.

8. DIY Dish Planter Dangling of Pleated

This gorgeous patterned Umbra dish is ideal for building a DIY planter dangling. You may utilize whatever dish you have well. A simple jar will fit for that one. Only build the dangler from twine rope and Bind it to your house's ceiling or on the covered roof or porch.

8. Beautiful DIY Water Garden Dangling

A dangling planter does not actually carry any other plants in the building. You can build a beautiful dangling water garden that can provide you the greenery you desire and put a truly unique feel to space. For this reason, a revamped fish tank is ideal, and you may install any water plant you desire. Stones and other decorations give it a very good look, and you can bring this one together in simply five minutes.

9. DIY Bindred Planter Dangling

A few planters of wire in some paint and various widths are simply about what you want to make this beautiful DIY dangling Bindred plantings. In case you have some wired baskets, you may add as many thirds as you like. To offer them a completely special appearance, you may paint them in various kinds of colors and put beads and other decorations. This is very simple and good for getting different plants that you desire to put.

10. DIY Pansy Ball Dangling

A dangling floral ball can be a lovely way to bring much color to every space in your house. This is created from pansies and put together is super simple. You don't see planter anyway. You simply see a pretty flower ball that you may hang from either outdoors or indoors. You create it from two inexpensive dangling basketball planters, then bring them close to create a ball shape.

11. Reused Embroidery Hoop Planter Dangling

I adore this reused planter with the embroidery. You may create these with the size of the embroidery hoop you have at present, considering your plant or dish suits inside it. It can be a very beautiful dangling planter and makes it very simple. In case you have any old dishes to reuse, you may utilize them and render it a fully repurposed planting project.

12. DIY Dangling of Wooden Shelf

This dangling planter is constructed from a plate of wood and has a gorgeous rustic feel to it. In case you don't have a plate which you may utilize, well, if you got the proper equipment, you can easily make one yourself. Then you only have to pick something to attach with – string, twine, and so on – then put planter to the disc made of wood.

13. Revamped Tire Dangling Planter

The old tire you found in the lawn will make a great planter. Well, there're many styles you may revamp used tires, and my favorites are this one. You're simply dangling the tire from a tree and attaching the plant to it – yeah, there's a little more effort involved than that, but it's a really simple and imaginative idea.

14. DIY Jar (Mason) Planter Dangling

I love projects with a mason jar, really. Each one is too simple to build and so beautiful when it's finished. You can need a vacant jar to build a plant and then cover it with cords, or if you like the rustic feel of the farmhouse, you might use twine. For small plants, this is a perfect project as well as you may hang these jars indoors or outdoors.

15. DIY Ball Planter of Moss Dangling

These ball planters can be very good and simple to make. In reality, it is the best and least costly DIY dangling planters you might make. To build it, you need simply dirt, some cords, and moss, obviously your chosen vine. With these or also tiny flowering plants, you might do succulents so you will render your moose balls as tiny or as big as you want them.

16. Reused Inverted Planters Dangling

Well, I do love those dangling inverted planters. They're so amusing and look amazing on the deck or inside your house. These are really simple to produce, and you use recycled products to build them, so they're pretty cheap too. It can be a perfect idea to repurpose some hollow coffee containers, or if you like them to be a little bigger, you might utilize tin cans or 2 Liter bottles.

17. Revamped Plastic Bottle Planters Dangling

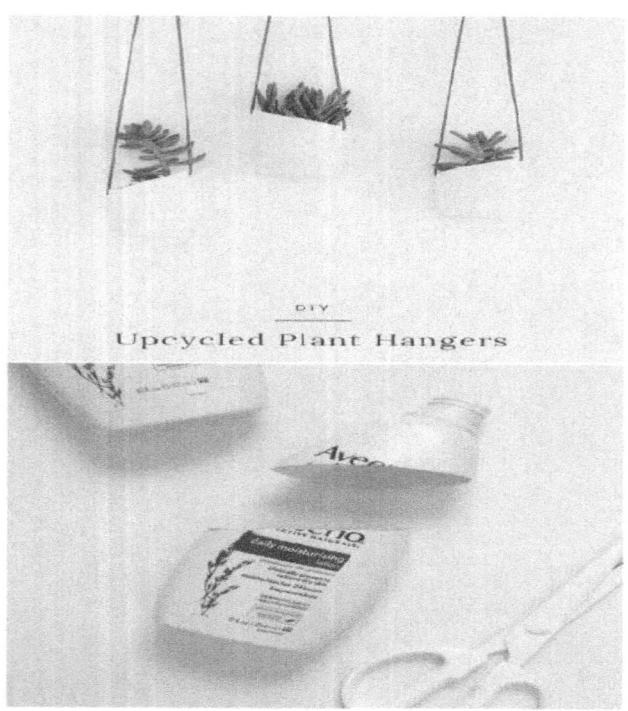

We all know these used bottles of shampoo, conditioner, and lotion you put out whenever they are vacant? Can we turn these in a beautiful dangling planter? As these are really simple, and they are also super cheap to make as you're utilizing vacant bottles. To make them attractive, you'll need to cut these bottles a little and cover or paint them up. However, it can be a very simple project, and also these might happen to be some great gifts.

18. Dangling of Wooden Basket Planter

A few lightweight baskets can be turned into elegant dangling planters. And, you can only check out those gorgeous ones I find on Etsy. They're really inexpensive, around 10 dollars each of them, and you only put the plants on the deck once you get them. You may also use such in house, and they also have a beautiful rustic look, which is ideal for decorating your farmhouse.

19. Dangling of Wooden Pendant Planter

To decorate any room in your house, create these gorgeous pendant dangling planters. These are very easy to produce and look so lovely and special to them. And you may utilize them to grow smaller plants such as some small plants which don't require much space. I can be an ideal approach to put some color to the house, and you're literally not going to admit how much easy it is to produce.

Conclusion

The macramé truly has endless possibilities of knots, patterns, and a combination of two. This is one of the reasons it can be addicting, and once you fall in love with the craft, your ideas will be endless. In every project, you will learn a new technique, approach or idea to begin thinking outside of the box. It is guaranteed that everyone who loves this craft to go beyond these projects will come up with unique and original ideas. I hope some of these concepts will get you excited and bursting with ideas to try.

You can change the look of any project or design simply by changing the spacing of knots. Any pattern changes completely when you tie the rows very close together versus leaving space between them. For example, the final look of alternating square knots is completely changed by the amount of spacing between them. Have fun adjusting the spacing between rows and knots to vary designs to your individual style. Another way to change the look of the project is by changing the color of rope, adding a color rope, or dying your rope. Another method is to alter your macramé project is by adding layers to create depth. This idea can be applied to any type of project.

It is always helpful to think about pairing intricate patterns with simple ones, or by playing with negative and positive space. Negative space is just as important as the knots and patterns in your piece because it makes both spaces more impactful.

Go to knots and pattern section for more tips on how to expand beyond each specific pattern and try combining different patterns in one piece.

I hope you feel inspired to create your own unique macramé pieces using some of the concepts. Don't forget to experiment and try new ideas.

References

Sewing, T.. An Introduction to Macramé Knotting. Retrieved, from https://feltmagnet.com/textiles-sewing/An-Introduction-to-Macrame-Knotting

A fascinating macramé history Retrieved, from https://www.hunker.com/13712633/the-history-of-macrame-is-in-fact-fascinating

How to Macrame: Tools You'll Need to Get Started - Macramé Lovers Blog., from http://www.macramelovers.com/blog/macrame-cord/tools-started-macrame/

How to Macrame., from https://www.wikihow.com/Macrame

Burt, P. Discover our library of macramé knots - Mollie Makes. Retrieved, from http://www.molliemakes.com/stitch-library/library-macrame-knots/

Macrame Patterns You Can Make Today. Retrieved from https://www.thesprucecrafts.com/free-macrame-patterns-4177826

How to Display Macrame Decor in Your Home. Retrieved, from https://www.thespruce.com/throwback-ways-to-display-macrame-4148457

Fresh, F. Chic Macramé Wall Hanging DIY for Beginners - FTD.com. Retrieved, from https://www.ftd.com/blog/create/macrame-wall-hanging

Pretty Macrame Plant Hanger Patterns for Beginners. Retrieved, from https://www.thesprucecrafts.com/beginner-plant-hanger-patterns-4768729

How to Macrame a Purse. Retrieved, from https://thisyearsdozen.wordpress.com/2008/05/18/how-to-macrame-a-purse/

Made in the USA
Monee, IL
04 November 2020